THE FAITH WE AFFIRM

Basic Beliefs of Disciples of Christ

THE FAITH WE AFFIRM

Basic Beliefs
of Disciples of Christ

RONALD E. OSBORN

The Bethany Press

St. Louis, Missouri

Third Printing, April 1983

Library of Congress cataloging in Publication Data

Osborn, Ronald E.
      The faith we affirm.
      1. Christian Church (Disciples of Christ)—Doctrinal and controversial works—Christian Church (Disciples of Christ) authors.
      2. Christian education—Text-books for adults—Christian Church (Disciples of Christ) I. Title.
      BX7321.2.082   230'.6'6   79-21079
      ISBN 0-8272-1009-4

Printed in the U.S.A.

Distributed in Canada by The G. R. Welch Company, Ltd.
Toronto, Ontario, Canada

CONTENTS

Editor's Foreword

Members of the Christian Church (Disciples of Christ), in this last quarter of the twentieth century, have manifested a renewed interest in exploring the basic beliefs which shape our witness to the Christian faith. As we broaden our ecumenical involvements and reflect on the history through which God has led us, we also seek to enlarge our vision of the mission to which God calls the church in our time.

It is in response to repeated requests for a study guide to assist us in our quest that this book is offered. Its primary purpose is to engage Disciples in thinking responsibly about the faith we affirm in the light of our heritage and in the context of our contemporary situation.

The faith we affirm as Disciples is succinctly set forth in the first paragraph of the Preamble to *The Design for the Christian Church (Disciples of Christ)*. Phrases from this affirmation which appears on pages 8 and 9 are used as chapter headings, and statements from it serve to introduce each chapter. This study is offered as a replacement for an earlier course, *Doctrine and Thought of the Disciples of Christ,* by Howard E. Short, which is no longer in print.

The author of *The Faith We Affirm,* Ronald E. Osborn, is a distinguished teacher and writer whose personal faith is deeply rooted in this tradition. He was the first moderator of the church in 1968 and is a frequent lecturer at ministers' institutes and church assemblies. This volume represents a lifetime of reflection on the Disciples witness. His major interest is in motivating us to seek a more mature faith with understanding.

This book is designed both for individual reading and for use with study groups of youth and adults, especially participants in church membership classes. By devoting a session to each chapter, a group may complete the study in six sessions. However, each chapter provides sufficient content for two or more sessions, furnishing a resource for as much as an entire quarter's study.

While no session plans are developed here, questions at the end of each chapter may provide topics which participants will want to explore in their group sessions.

For more information about our heritage and how our church operates, the following resources will be useful. *Journey in Faith: A History of the Christian Church (Disciples of Christ)* by William E. Tucker and Lester G. McAllister (Bethany Press, 1975) offers a comprehensive history of the Disciples. For a description of how the church is organized and functions see *We Call Ourselves Disciples* by Kenneth L. Teegarden (Bethany Press, 1975). The document outlining how our life together is ordered, *The Design for the Christian Church (Disciples of Christ),* is printed in our church's *Year Book and Directory* for 1979. Separate copies of *The Design* (73A1708, 25¢) also are available from Christian Board of Publication.

The affirmation of faith, which this study invites us to explore, is used today by many congregations in their common worship of God. (It is No. 490 in the *Hymnbook for Christian Worship.*) A careful reading of this book should enable worshipers to have a better understanding of the faith which is being affirmed.

Herschell H. Richmond

An Affirmation of Faith

AS MEMBERS OF THE CHRISTIAN CHURCH,

We confess that Jesus is the Christ,
     the Son of the living God,
     and proclaim him Lord and Savior of the world.

In Christ's name and by his grace
     we accept our mission of witness
     and service to all people.

We rejoice in God,
     maker of heaven and earth,
     and in the covenant of love
     which binds us to God and one another.

Through baptism into Christ
     we enter into newness of life
     and are made one with the whole people of God.

In the communion of the Holy Spirit
  we are joined together in discipleship
  and in obedience to Christ.

At the table of the Lord
  we celebrate with thanksgiving
  the saving acts and presence of Christ.

Within the universal church
  we receive the gift of ministry
  and the light of scripture.

In the bonds of Christian faith
  we yield ourselves to God
  that we may serve the One
  whose kingdom has no end.

Blessing, glory and honor
  be to God forever. Amen.

—From the Preamble of the
*Design for the Christian Church
(Disciples of Christ).*

We confess that Jesus is the Christ,
the Son of the living God . . .
Within the universal church
we receive . . . the light of scripture.

1

THE LIGHT OF SCRIPTURE

The Bible as Interpreted by Disciples

BECAUSE the sublime language of the Bible proclaims religious faith, many persons—both inside and outside the church— apparently do not know what to make of it. Faith to them has to do with feeling, with miracle, with mystery. They conclude therefore that a testimony of religious belief must necessarily be irrational, or beyond understanding. Some who are outside the church imagine that faith cannot stand up under critical examination.

Some persons who are inside the church hold a strikingly similar view. Any attempt to submit the Bible or a creed to analysis by contemporary thought, they fear, is irreverent. Some even suppose that if they could explain their convictions in rational terms, they would no longer "truly believe." They identify religion with mystery.

Disciples of Christ, however, link understanding with faith. The word *disciple,* used so frequently in the New Testament, means both *learner* and *follower,* one who accompanied a traveling teacher. It refers to a person whose faith imparts insight, understanding, and guidance for living. Consequently, this faith evokes dedication: a disciple of Jesus is an adherent. But commitment is not separated from comprehension. Rather, each intensifies the other. (Discipleship will be explored in more detail in chapter 5.)

Faith, Scripture, and Understanding

Here we are focusing on a cast of mind which holds faith and understanding together. It is this link which enables the disciple to think responsibly about Christian beliefs from the Scriptures. To receive "the light of scripture" requires us to have respect for our minds.

Because the Bible addresses our entire being, it speaks not only to our hearts, but also to our minds to evoke understanding. It has inspired a long tradition of respect for human intelligence in the service of God. The prophet Isaiah offered this counsel: "Come now, let us reason together, says the LORD" (Isa. 1:18). In stating the commandment which takes priority, Jesus stated that persons are to "love the Lord your God . . . with all your mind" (Mark 12:30).

Christians today are heirs of a noble tradition of intellectual activity. St. Augustine, in the fourth century, described the action of theology as "faith seeking understanding." The early leaders of the Disciples of Christ contended for a faith characterized as sane, scriptural, and practical. They were motivated by a faith which, to them, "made sense."

Disciples who want to understand the faith will undertake to enlarge both their knowledge and comprehension. The house of faith will be illuminated by understanding, as the light of scripture streams in. It will have great clerestory windows to flood all its space with brightness and warmth from above.

It was in just such a manner that Alexander Campbell wanted the Bible to illuminate the life of the church and the minds of the people. For this reason he published a fresh translation of the New Testament by a group of British scholars. Commonly known by its binder's title, *The Living Oracles,* this translation pioneered the principle of rendering the Scriptures in modern speech so that readers may more readily understand.

Moreover, Campbell insisted, with stubborn conviction, on the use of the term "disciple" to designate a follower of Christ. Other early leaders, such as Barton W. Stone and Walter Scott, deemed the name "Christian" more fitting. Because of Campbell's persistence, we have been so compelled to call ourselves Disciples that we stagger awkwardly under our official name, Christian Church (Disciples of Christ). Thus we sometimes refer to ourselves as "The People of the Parentheses."

The intent of Campbell's choice of the name for a people committed to Christ was to emphasize that we are all *learners*. The faith of Christ's adherents is a matter of growing understanding and of thinking about the Bible.

An archbishop from Yugoslavia, who did not know English, once visited Christian Theological Seminary. He knew our name in German, *die Junger Christi,* and his translator had him addressing us as "Jesus's Pupils." We smile. But that is precisely the point of the name *disciple;* we are learners.

Many people do not seem to know about the biblical kinship between faith and wisdom. They have not heard about loving God with all the mind. There is much ignorance of the Bible and the basic tenets of the Christian faith. Even to some persons inside the churches, the biblical vocabulary sounds like an alien tongue.

Confused as to what the Bible teaches, what the church professes, or what they themselves believe, some people turn to the brightly colored tents of the hucksters. They put their faith in all kinds of religion, psychology, or pure hokum. On television and in huge tabernacles, some evangelists hawk an anti-intellectual notion of the gospel which offers certainty at the price of a throttled mind. "It's in the Book!" they shout. Or, "The Bible says!" That ends it.

Today, a simplistic, distorted version of Christianity has rushed in to fill an intellectual vacuum. Recently, in a meeting of Disciples from across the land, we heard reports of a proof-texting kind of biblicism everywhere, even in our own congregations. We seem to have raised up a generation which no longer thinks with the Disciples mind.

The Mind of Disciples

What do we mean by the Disciples mind? It is a way of approaching the Scriptures with a reverent intelligence. This style of professing Christian faith has accepted the reproach of advocating a "head religion" hurled by those who profess a "heart religion."

Emphasizing faith with understanding, the Disciples mind puts the highest premium on rationality and faithfulness in action. This faith is biblically based, but it is understood in the light of scripture.

While the Disciples mind is *biblical,* it is more than that. It is *reasonable:* it thinks the Bible through with common sense. It is *empirical:* it reads the Bible in light of the knowledge that comes through the sciences. It is *pragmatic:* it tests in action the teachings of scripture and all religious notions.

BY TRIAL AND ERROR

Reasonable, empirical, pragmatic—these three characteristics are more fully described by the late W. B. Blakemore in *The Reformation of Tradition,* edited by Ronald E. Osborn (Bethany Press, 1963). To this list, we would add *ecumenical:* the Disciples mind seeks biblical understanding in light of the common mind of the whole church.

We will now consider each of the elements in this five-part process, beginning with the Bible.

A Biblical Mind

Thomas Campbell, in the *Declaration and Address,* declared: "Where the Scriptures speak, we speak; where the Scriptures are silent, we are silent." What is the meaning of this slogan?

• The Bible conveys a knowledge of God. It makes known to us the Awesome but Friendly Presence who dwelt with our primordial ancestors at the early dawn of the human race. In it we hear the Voice of Promise who called Abraham and Sarah to a unique mission. Here we behold the Divine Emancipator who, by the hand of Moses, led a people out of slavery and claimed them in holy covenant. Here we listen to the One Altogether Holy who spoke to Israel through priest and prophet, poet and sage, holy women and holy men of many generations.

Moreover, in the Bible we meet the Forgiving Parent who, in heaven's supreme act of self-revelation, made divinity known to us in a human life, in Jesus of Nazareth. Here we encounter the Redemptive Power whose holy Spirit enabled Jesus' followers to proclaim the good news of the risen Christ and to establish a church committed to the gospel. Across the centuries, the Bible has spoken this great story.

The church, from its earliest days, has called the Bible the Word of God. Through its writings God speaks to us. Not that God gives us orders through these ancient texts, but that the same God who confronted the people of long ago now confronts us as we ponder their story. To understand God and the shape of the Christian life, we go to the Bible for light.

14

• Christians therefore need to know the Bible. To deal with the issues of faith and life today, we must have enough familiarity with scripture to draw on its resources. Some of our early Disciples ancestors were nicknamed "walking Bibles." Walter Scott maintained that anyone considered for the office of deacon in the church should be expected to know the New Testament by heart. It was said of J. W. McGarvey, president of one of our seminaries, that if all the Bibles in the world were destroyed, he could reproduce the text from memory. This is probably an exaggeration, but at least he could recite great portions of it.

A mind described as biblical loves the scriptures. Learning to know them is one way of serving God.

• As we come to know the Bible, we discover in it striking developments across vast periods of time. Alexander Campbell, in his "Sermon of the Law," noted that the law given through Moses was binding on Israel, but that Christians belong to a new dispensation. The church, therefore, is not under the Mosaic law. Rather Christians base their lives on the witness of the apostles to Jesus Christ. It is their teachings and practices which direct the church. Those who claim to take the Bible seriously must use it with discrimination.

• Alexander Campbell spoke proudly of his position as "true Bibleism." By this he meant that the church should pattern its life and teaching after the essentials of Christianity as set forth in the New Testament. Any requirements the church might make on its members which are not clearly set forth in the New Testament should be eliminated.

Campbell also insisted on using "Bible words" to talk about "Bible things." He disliked the language of traditional theology which he regarded as too technical and abstract, in sharp contrast to the vivid speech of Jesus and the plain words of the apostles. He refused to use such terms as trinity and sacrament. He felt that any Christian who comes to the Bible with an honest mind can understand it without the interpretation of a priest, bishop, or theologian.

• The biblical commitment of the Disciples mind tended to shape the practices in the congregations. They called themselves by biblical names: Disciples, Christians, Christian Church, Church of Christ. They undertook to restore the faith and order of the apostolic church. They insisted on believer's baptism which they viewed as normative in the earliest church. They practiced immersion as the baptismal form, convinced that it was clearly taught in the New Testament. For the same reason they observed the Lord's supper every Lord's Day.

• Across the generations, many Disciples have demanded a prooftext for everything that was done or taught. They called this a "thus saith the Lord." As a result, they fell into a new legalism, making the words of the Bible into a creed. Most Disciples, however, have avoided this trap. We seek the light of scripture with a mind that is reasonable, empirical, and pragmatic.

A Reasonable Mind

Disciples have taken pride in advocating a common sense religion. We seek an approach which is sane as well as biblical, rational as well as practical. Here is an understanding of the faith which our pioneer leaders felt could be readily explained to ordinary folk, and which they could embrace with their intelligence as well as their hearts. Sometimes we have made our little systems too tight, too simple. But the genius of the Disciples mentality has held that we do not love God as we ought unless we examine the claims of religion with rational minds.

This commitment to reason, however, does not eliminate all mystery from life. Daily we confront realities beyond our powers of comprehension, such as beauty, evil, death, and God. Faith bows in reverence and humility before wonders too deep to fathom. Yet Disciples do not make a virtue of not understanding. A doctrine is not made sacred simply because it may be incomprehensible. Disciples insist that the gospel is intended by God to be understood, and that when we read the Scriptures reasonably they can be understood.

We Disciples, as we often remind ourselves, came into being in the wake of the Enlightenment movement of the eighteenth century. This fact noticeably affected the temper of our thought. The Reformation, from which most Protestant churches originated, marked the climax of the Middle Ages. The Enlightenment ushered in the modern era. Our Disciples founders lived with the great minds of the Age of Reason. They were acquainted with John Locke, the Scottish common sense philosophers, and American intellectuals such as Jefferson, Adams, and Franklin.

The early Disciples championed the faith in debate with skeptics, agnostics, and infidels. Alexander Campbell took on the celebrated Robert Owen to defend the cause of revealed religion. He also debated with religious leaders such as the Roman Catholic Bishop

Purcell with whom he contested the claims of hierarchical authority. From such intellectual contests the Disciples developed a polemic approach to doctrinal preaching and a skeptical cast of mind. They regarded ignorance and superstition as evils from which the gospel grants deliverance.

From this reasonable point of view a religious claim is not necessarily good simply because its proponents are sincere or feel good about it. It must stand scrutiny for truth and for ethical responsibility. It is not enough for preachers to teach people to have faith. They need to teach believers to raise questions about the faith they affirm. It is crucial that we Disciples continue to emphasize this aspect of our heritage.

In the classic formulations of the Disciples position, faith has two aspects. Basically, it means a personal commitment to Jesus Christ as Lord, and a continuing life as a disciple of Jesus. But faith also has a substantive side. It is a body of beliefs. These beliefs, however, are not to be professed simply out of emotion, nor to be accepted merely on the assertion of some authority. Faith is expressed by confessing Christian belief out of intellectual conviction. It is arrived at on the basis of evidence presented in the scriptures.

A belief that the Bible, when it is rightly read, makes sense and ought to make sense has been a major emphasis of the Disciples. They have imputed integrity to the mind of God. Occasionally we may encounter persons who exalt divine authority above divine wisdom. Some have even said, with great unction: "If the Bible commanded me to run my head into a stone wall, I would do it!" Disciples, however, maintain that God as revealed in Jesus Christ is never arbitrary or capricious. They point to the Great Commandment which bids us to love God with our minds.

Nevertheless, Disciples sometimes forget this cardinal principle. Some used to urge that, because scripture says an elder or deacon must be "the husband of one wife" (1 Tim. 3:2, 12, KJV), only married persons may stand for these offices. One British brother insisted that if an elder's wife died, he must resign at once because he would no longer be eligible. Most Disciples, reading this passage with common sense, see it simply as a prohibition of polygamy. In many of our congregations today, this passage is understood also to mean that an elder may be "the wife of one husband."

One of Alexander Campbell's major contributions to our Disciples heritage was the set of rules for a reasonable interpretation of the Bible which he popularized. These were not his own invention, but he did make available to congregations principles with which responsible biblical scholars had been working since the Renaissance and Protestant Reformation. These rules were published in *The Christian System* (chap. 2).

Campbell suggested that the reader, on opening any book of the Bible, should consider the historical circumstances of its writing, such as author, date, place, and occasion. Also we should observe who is speaking, to whom it is addressed, and the message it is intended to convey. In regard to interpretation, the same rules should be applied to its language as would be applied to the language of any other book.

In discerning the message of a biblical writing, Campbell suggested that the meaning of any word should always be decided on the basis of common usage. For words which have more than one meaning, the precise meaning should be decided by the context or use in parallel passages. The interpretation of figurative language, symbols, and parables in the Scriptures follows the same pattern used in interpreting these literary devices in secular writings.

The final rule stated by Campbell is that the reader seek to come within "the understanding distance" of the scriptures. He was convinced that the Bible was intended for our edification, and, with diligent seeking, we should be able to understand it.

In order to produce informed and thinking Christians, capable of reading the Bible with understanding and applying its precepts to their lives, the Disciples pioneers founded colleges across the land. These were liberal arts schools for teaching students to think and become responsible persons in society rather than seminaries for training a professional clergy. Here students were prepared to pursue careers as educators, doctors, lawyers, editors, and entrepreneurs while they also were being equipped intellectually to serve as elders, deacons, and teachers in the church.

The Disciples mind is both biblical and reasonable. We are convinced that God intends the Bible to make sense.

An Empirical Mind

The Disciples mind is also empirical. It reads the Bible reasonably in the light of modern secular knowledge. All of the empirical studies—from astronomy, physics, chemistry, geology, biology, psychology, on through geography, archaeology, anthropology, sociology, and history—are pertinent to a Christian's thinking. We cannot read the Bible as though we had never heard of Copernicus or Darwin, Marx or Freud, Albert Einstein or Margaret Mead. Hearing the Scriptures today necessarily involves a dialogue between two worlds, the world of the Bible and the contemporary world.

The Disciples founders cut their intellectual teeth on the writings of John Locke, the empirical philosopher who maintained that all verifiable knowledge comes to us through the senses. Alexander Campbell accepted this principle, even for religion. The gospel, he insisted, consists of facts to be believed, a series of historical events accessible to observation. He may have oversimplified or over-rationalized, but his empirical commitment is clear.

Many religious people, in the mid-nineteenth century, became agitated when geologists spoke of certain features of the earth being shaped by processes that required millions of years. Ministers often promoted debates on "Geology or Genesis?" A young Disciples preacher, James A. Garfield, who later was elected President of the United States, defended the scientific point of view. Another Disciples minister, Alexander Procter, gained national attention in the news media for espousing evolution in his preaching.

Disciples also carried empiricism into the realm of faith. Many people ask: How do you know you are saved? Disciples insist that religious assurance is not a matter of feeling. Rather they contend that God has promised salvation to all who confess Jesus Christ and are baptized in faith and repentance. The highest form of spiritual experience offered by Christian faith is positive and objective, rather than mystical and charismatic. It centers in a public act, a corporate act, a visible action—the breaking of bread by the congregation gathered about the Lord's table.

Some views advanced by our Disciples founders, however, are no longer adequate for us. These rested on assumptions long since proved false. What is important for us is the honesty of their minds, their reasonable and pragmatic temper, rather than their conclusions, which we must correct in the light of new data.

They considered the New Testament, for example, as the divinely given constitution for the church. Thus they assumed that it must reflect a uniformity of faith and practice. They supposed that what they read about the church in Antioch applied equally to the churches in Jerusalem or Rome, or that congregations at the end of the first century operated in the same way as did the disciples immediately following Pentecost. They missed the many splendored diversity of New Testament life.

More careful empirical study now makes clear the striking variety in early Christian theology and practice. Congregations did not do everything alike in Judea, in Samaria, and in the uttermost parts of the earth. As the decades rolled by, they worked out new ways of doing things. To speak responsibly of a New Testament church, we need to recognize the diversity in the various Christian communities. The oneness of the church derives from the one Lord, not from uniformity of practice.

Like our Disciples pioneers, we need to continue to study the Bible empirically. We are not being unfaithful to the scriptures by reading them honestly in the light of facts established since they were written. To look at the Bible without trying to forget what we now know is a part of our heritage of common sense.

A Pragmatic Mind

Another aspect of the Disciples mind is the conviction that we learn from experience. It is pragmatic. This means that we put our beliefs to a practical test in our own lives, in our congregations, and in the larger life of the church. On the basis of this experience, we revise our previous understanding of what the Bible seeks to tell us.

Jesus warned his disciples to beware of false teachers, insisting, "You will know them by their fruits" (Matt. 7:20). This same pragmatic principle is illustrated in Jesus' statement that if it is our will to do God's will, we "shall know whether the teaching is from God" (John 7:17). Alexander Campbell has been quoted as saying, "Nothing can be Christian doctrine that cannot be translated into life."

Disciples have taken as much pride in calling their faith practical as in calling it reasonable. Their pragmatic approach to biblical teaching began to show itself very early.

They started out trying to order the life of their churches in strict accordance with the New Testament. But they soon discovered that the Bible is silent on many matters. It doesn't tell us how many elders a congregation should have. It does not say how often we should elect members to the official board or how many should be on the board. (In fact, it does not even mention an "official board.") Neither does it tell us how to arrange an order of worship, or how long the sermon should be ("sermon" is not a scriptural term either).

Soon Disciples began to speak about the "law of expediency." This meant that congregations have to use common sense and reflect on the lessons of experience. When the scriptures point to something we ought to do, but do not tell us how to do it, congregations need to decide on a course of action which seems most expedient.

20

Resorting to the law of expediency, congregations developed organizational patterns: committees, specific offices, the church school, organizations for women, for youth, for men. In our general life we used it to justify missionary societies and various agencies and institutions to carry out the work of the churches. More recently, pragmatic thinking guided the shaping of our shared life together in *The Design for the Christian Church (Disciples of Christ)*. By mutual consent our people, in 1968, adopted this organizational structure in order to be both more responsible and effective in our witness to the gospel in the world today.

An Ecumenical Mind

In describing the particular cast of mind of the Disciples of Christ we do not want to seem boastful or partisan. Disciples resist any tendency toward a sectarian emphasis. Our intention is to read the biblical message in the light of the common judgment of the whole Christian community and for the sake of the whole church.

We Disciples did not decide which books belong in the Bible. The ancient catholic church decided that. In their judgment at that point we concur. So we must give heed, insofar as we are able, to the judgment of the best minds in all the churches across the centuries in regard to the meaning of scripture.

Disciples have insisted on the right of every Christian to read the Bible for oneself. Over against this right, however, we have balanced the admonition: "No prophecy of scripture is a matter of one's own interpretation" (2 Peter 1:20). We need to listen to the "common mind" of the church before we make up our own individual minds.

Alexander Campbell was unwilling to base his practice on what he regarded as unscriptural practice in other churches. Nevertheless, he gave careful attention to the work of other religious leaders in their study of the Bible. It is this stance which is reflected in our Affirmation of Faith: "Within the universal church we receive . . . the light of scripture."

The Bible is an ecumenical book. To read it rightly, we must read it ecumenically. When we read it rightly, it will make us ecumenical. Disciples have sought for themselves, and for all Christians everywhere, an ecumenical mind.

21

Dialogue with Scripture

The fivefold mode of thinking which has characterized Disciples involves us in a dynamic dialogue with the Scriptures. The Bible is a vast library of testimonies to the reality of God. Many people across the centuries have been inspired to tell the story of Israel's encounters with Yahweh, and of God's supreme revelation in the person of Jesus whom we call the Christ. Many others have undertaken to offer directions for living based on their understanding of God's will in their particular situations.

Each of the accounts—in narrative, law, psalm, proverb, gospel, epistle—comes from a particular time and addresses a particular circumstance. Not all of them rise to the same level of understanding, nor do all of them agree. Yet they all testify to the living God. For this reason the community of faith—first Jewish, then Christian—has acknowledged them as part of the canon of sacred scripture. It sets the standard for the faith we profess.

In our interpretation of the Bible today we will not always come to the same conclusions as earlier generations of Disciples. The intense biblical scholarship of almost two centuries since Barton W. Stone and the Campbells began their work has given us a clearer understanding of many parts of scripture that was not available to them. However, we are being faithful to the Disciples mind when we take the Bible seriously, read it in the light of contemporary knowledge, and reflect on its message for our present situation.

Biblical, reasonable, empirical, pragmatic, ecumenical—by persisting in the use of these principles, we can carry on an enriching dialogue with the Bible. Thus, "we receive the light of scripture."

For Reflection and Discussion

What do you understand to be the nature of the Bible? In what sense do you personally regard it as God's *word* for Christian living?

What is your understanding of how God communicates with us through the scriptures? In what ways do you seek the light of scripture on specific issues which call for a decision?

What do you understand to be the meaning of faith? What is the relationship between faith and a personal commitment of our lives to God?

What authority does the Bible have for Christian living? What would be your response if someone should ask you, "How do we decide which parts of the Bible are authoritative for us today?"

What suggestions could you offer someone who wants to find out what the Bible says about a specific problem?

Can you think of any particular problems for which the scriptures offer no precise answers? If so, how would you decide what is the right thing to do in such situations?

What is your understanding of how persons are to "love the Lord your God . . . with all your mind" (Mark 12:30)? How does loving God with our minds influence the way we think and what we do as Christians?

In this chapter, the author describes the Disciples mind as being biblical, reasonable, empirical, pragmatic, and ecumenical. To what extent do you regard these five principles as a valid approach for interpreting the scriptures?

Reflect on the affirmation that "within the universal church we receive . . . the light of scripture." To what extent do you listen to the "common mind" of the church for guidance in formulating your own interpretation of the scriptures?

How important is it for a disciple of Jesus to know the Bible and study it regularly? What, precisely, does it mean to *know* the Bible?

What new insights have you received from this chapter in regard to how Disciples of Christ have interpreted the Bible? To what extent has this discussion been helpful to you for seeking the light of scripture for your own understanding of the Christian life?

We confess that Jesus is the Christ,
the Son of the living God,
and proclaim him Lord and Savior
of the world. . . .
Through baptism into Christ
we enter into newness of life
and are made one with the whole
people of God.

2

JESUS CHRIST THE LORD

Meaning of the Good Confession

IF YOU are like most of the Disciples of Christ, the memory of one particular day stands out in your religious life. That was the day when you stood before the congregation and, taking your minister by the hand, you confessed your faith in Jesus as the Christ, the Son of the living God.

From the beginning, Disciples have believed that this confession of faith, by a responsible believer, properly precedes baptism. It is fitting, therefore, that this study of the faith we affirm should begin with Jesus Christ and the beliefs which Disciples have cherished in regard to him.

In making our profession of faith, most of us have repeated or assented to a form of words much like the following:

I believe that Jesus is the Christ, the Son of the Living God, and I take him as Lord of my life.

Disciples call this "the good confession," a phrase found in 1 Timothy 6:12. The first line recasts in confessional form the words of Peter's confession, "You are the Christ, the Son of the living God" (Matt. 16:16). The second line echoes the confession of Thomas: "My Lord and my God!" (John 20:28).

In some congregations, the second line of this confessional formula is changed to "and I take him as my personal Savior." But this form of words has no foundation in any confession found in the New Testament. Rather it reflects the language of pietistic revivalism which was prominent in American churches during the past century. Even today the phrase "personal Savior" appears so frequently in Protestant devotion that for many persons it expresses the essence of Christian faith.

If this phrase is to be used in the confessional formula, we need to be clear about what is meant by it. If the person making the confession means that "I personally take Christ as Savior," that would be in harmony with biblical thought. For the biblical faith is intensely personal. But the expression, "personal Savior," as widely understood, works to privatise Christian faith. It suggests that Christ's saving work deals primarily with the inner spiritual concerns of individuals. Used in this sense, the phrase "personal Savior" contradicts the very meaning of Savior, and also of Christ and Lord.

Christ, Lord, Savior—these three terms are all public titles having to do with the common life shared by a people. In making our confession, it is best to phrase it to say precisely what we mean. This is what Disciples attempt to do in the affirmation the church makes in regard to Jesus: "We . . . proclaim him Lord and Savior of the world."

Whatever variations may be used, however, the words of Peter's confession, as recorded in Matthew, have claimed the hearts of Disciples from the beginning. This affirmation of faith has always been deemed a sufficient statement, theologically speaking, to qualify a person for baptism and membership in the church.

Disciples recognize, of course, that what we mean when we affirm our faith in Jesus is more important than the formula we use to express it. Not everyone who makes the good confession fully understands what it means. Indeed, does anyone ever fully understand? Certainly Simon Peter did not at the time he confessed Jesus as the Christ. When Jesus began to talk about going to Jerusalem and suffering and being killed, Peter rebuked him, saying, "God forbid, Lord! This shall never happen to you" (Matt. 16:22).

At that point in his development as a disciple, Peter apparently thought of Jesus as a messianic leader who would use miraculous power to drive out Israel's enemies and solve the nation's ills. Hailing Jesus as the Christ (Messiah) amounted to trying to co-opt the power of God for his own purposes. Some people's understanding still moves on that level. Often we have heard someone say, "Christ is the answer!" implying that if we truly believe and trust in him, he will solve all of our problems.

If Simon Peter, the chief of the apostles, failed to understand Jesus, it should not surprise us that some would-be disciples today also misunderstand. The thought of Jesus' suffering and being killed, to Peter's mind, contradicted the very idea of the Christ. The notion today that God is present in our suffering to suffer with us denies the popular idea that religion will remove all obstacles to our success in the world.

The most shattering word Jesus ever spoke to a follower was his statement to Simon Peter, "Get behind me, Satan" (Matt. 16:23). The severity of that rebuke indicates the importance of what we are confessing when we affirm our belief that Jesus is the Christ. We need to examine carefully what this confession meant to the earliest Christians.

Earliest Confessions of Faith

The present order of the books in the New Testament does not follow the order in which they were written. The earliest documents are the letters of the apostle Paul. The Gospels, which tell of the life and teachings of Jesus, were written after Paul was gone from the scene. Thus our earliest written confession is the one which recurs throughout Paul's letters, the simple statement: "Jesus is Lord." This was the affirmation of faith used in the churches of the Gentiles which Paul established as a missionary to the pagans. They had only a limited knowledge of the Old Testament and the Jewish vocabulary of faith until they heard the preaching of the gospel.

The Gospel of Mark, written ten to twenty years after Paul's major letters, and the writings of John indicate an equally simple confession also professed in Jewish churches: "Jesus is the Christ." These Palestinian Christians, in contrast to the Gentiles, were deeply versed in the language of the Scriptures.

Thus we have in the New Testament two forms of confession, using two different titles: "Jesus is the Christ" and "Jesus is Lord." What did the early Christians mean when they affirmed their faith in Jesus, often at the peril of their lives?

"Jesus is the Christ"[1]

"Christ" *(Christos)* is a translation into Greek of the Hebrew word "Messiah." In English it would be translated "Anointed One." Anointing, in the Old Testament, was a sign that God had chosen a person for a public task. The high priest was anointed at the time of ordination to office. Commoners were anointed to be kings. (See 1 Sam. 10:1; 16:13.)

After the nation had been destroyed by the Babylonians (587 B.C.), devout Jews continued to believe that God would send yet another anointed leader to restore the glory of his people. But one humiliation followed another. First, the Syrians and then the Romans overran the land. Against the might of the occupation forces human resistance seemed hopeless.

Nevertheless, fanatical patriots called Zealots, launched a succession of rebellions. Some of these groups hailed their leaders as "Messiah." (See Acts 5:36-37.) Eventually these guerilla uprisings so provoked the Romans that they destroyed Jerusalem in A.D. 70. After one last rebellion, Roman legions obliterated the site of Jerusalem and completely banished the Jews from their homeland. They remained a people without a country until the founding of the modern state of Israel in 1948.

During these turbulent times many religious Jews came to believe in a supernatural Messiah. Every time a new uprising occurred, the Roman authorities reacted quickly to subdue the guerillas and execute their leaders by crucifixion. Consequently, many persons came to feel that only by divine intervention could the nation be restored. They expected God to send his Messiah, with legions of angels, to drive out their enemies and establish the divine reign (kingdom).

During Jesus' public ministry many people hailed him as Messiah. This caused great anxiety among the Roman authorities. After the procession into Jerusalem on Palm Sunday, they quickly placed Jesus under arrest. Then they crucified him as a rebel, as "King of the Jews." He died on a Roman cross in humiliation and agony.

---

[1] Typical references to this confession occur in Mark 8:29; 14:61-62; 1 John 5:1; John 7:41; 9:22; 11:27; Acts 9:22; 17:3.

Jesus' disciples, after witnessing his crucifixion and coming to believe in his resurrection, publicly proclaimed him as the Messiah. Those who believed the disciples' testimony began to make the incongruous confession, "*Jesus* is the Christ." Such an affirmation, on the face of it, was a contradiction.

Think what this meant: to proclaim that Jesus, a person without power who had died on a cross, is the Christ, God's Messiah! This confession compelled a total reversal in religious thinking; it was no longer possible to try to force Jesus into the mold of the popular messianic hope. (See John 6:15; Mark 10:35-37; Matt. 16:22.) He had turned all the old ideas upside down. Messiah must now be defined by the crucified Jesus. *He* is the Christ!

Jesus simply would not fit into anyone's religious expectations. Thus the Gospels turn everything around with the claim that he is Messiah. This was the highest title the evangelists knew to describe his uniqueness. Yet, even so, this title needed to be radically redefined.

This point is illustrated by the incident described in Matthew 11:2-6. From prison, John the Baptist sends his disciples to inquire of Jesus, "Are you the one who is to come, or shall we look for another?" Jesus replies, "Go and tell John what you hear and see: the blind receive their sight and the lame walk, lepers are cleansed and the deaf hear, and the dead are raised up, and the poor have good news preached to them. And blessed is he who takes no offense at me."

This response by Jesus is hardly a direct answer to the question John asked. He had no interest in claiming a title. He was saying, simply, "This is what I am doing. If you can think of Messiah in this way, then draw your own conclusion." But the Gospels, in describing Jesus' ministry, make it clear that the early Christians believed that Jesus is the Messiah (Christ) sent by God.

In affirming their faith in Jesus, the early Christians elaborated the simple form of confession in various ways. (Compare Luke 9:20; John 11:27; Matt. 16:16.) We need to keep in mind, however, that the meaning conveyed by each of these formulas was profoundly affected by the resurrection. The whole story was now known to the disciples. As Paul had stated, "We believe that Jesus died and rose again" (1 Thess. 4:14).

A form of confession which the apostle Paul had learned and taught in the churches he served goes like this:

[We believe]
that Christ died for our sins
in accordance with the scriptures,

that he was buried,
that he was raised on the third day
in accordance with the scriptures,
that he appeared to Cephas [Peter],
then to the twelve.
—1 Corinthians 15:3-5.

This helps us to understand what the earliest Christians were saying when they confessed Jesus as the Christ. They were insisting that he deserves the highest of titles which they knew, but that *he* defines what that title means. In the popular jargon of our time, they were saying, "Jesus is the most."

Is not this essentially what we mean when we make the good confession? It may be difficult for us to give a profound definition of Christ or Messiah. But we know about Jesus, and because of him, we look to God in faith and love. In effect, we are saying: In the deepest issues of our experience, in our purposes and hopes, in our needs and fears, in our loyalties and dreams, in life and in death, we trust completely in Jesus. We will follow where he leads us, and we will try to do his will in the world. For us, he is the most.

"Jesus Is Lord"

Reflect for a moment on how many pages it has taken us to ponder the meaning of the term *Christ*. As persons who call ourselves Disciples of Christ, we use this word countless times each week in worship. We hear it in sermons and in our church school classes. Some of us have read the New Testament, or at least the Gospels, many times. We confess our belief that "Jesus is the Christ." Yet we still find the term *Christ* not so easy to understand.

Imagine then that you are a first-century Christian. Your business has taken you from Palestine to Egypt, Greece, or Italy. There you establish contacts among the local populace. In time, a co-worker who gets to know you well notices that you follow a new faith. You do not worship any of the gods whose temples abound in these countries.

Your co-worker also notices that some of the people with whom you go to worship are not Jews, nor do they keep Jewish customs. This co-worker inquires about your faith. You mention the idea of one God, and that makes sense to your hearer. You talk about Jesus, and your friend is attracted by much that you say. Then you tell your friend, "We confess that Jesus is the Christ."

What could this possibly mean to your hearer? To a person who has never been to a synagogue, never read the Hebrew scriptures, or never heard of the messianic hope? Although *Christos* is a Greek word, it conveys no religious meaning to your friend. About the only meaning this term, referring to someone who is "annointed," could have for your friend is that Jesus is "smeared with oil."

Your friend presses you further, "But what does *Christ* mean? Then you answer, "Jesus is Lord."

Lord! (Greek, *Kyrios*). Now, this is a word your friend understands. Throughout the Greek-speaking world this term is a well-known title of respect and authority. It designates a person who is supreme in any relationship, such as an owner of property, the head of a household, a teacher among a group of disciples, a master of slaves, a boss of a business, a high government official, or the Roman Emperor. Used as a public title, *Lord* conveys the image of a person in authority over others.

Pious Jews also used this term in referring to God. They regarded the Hebrew name for God, Yahweh (Jehovah), as too sacred to pronounce. To avoid the frequent uttering of the divine name, they would make a substitution by saying, "the Lord."

The early Christians called Jesus *Lord*. When they used this term, they were referring to Jesus as having been put to death, risen, and ascended to heaven. It was a title of glory. (See Rom. 4:24-25; 14:7-9; 2 Cor. 4:14; 5:6-8.) They also used this title when speaking of their sense of Jesus' presence with them: "The Lord stood by me" (2 Tim. 4:17)

The earliest missionaries exhorted their hearers to "believe in the Lord Jesus" (Acts 16:31). New converts confessed "Jesus is Lord." Believers were baptized "in the name of the Lord Jesus" (Acts 19:5). Christians called their sacred meal the Lord's supper. In their worship, they prayed, "Come, Lord Jesus" (Rev. 22:20). They blessed one another with the benediction, "The grace of our Lord Jesus Christ be with you" (1 Thess. 5:28).

The title of *Lord* expressed the early Christians' conviction that Jesus exercised the supreme and exclusive sovereignty over their lives. Before long this got them into trouble. Since the Roman Emperor claimed the title of *Kyrios* (Lord) for himself, the Christian declaration, "Jesus is Lord," sounded like sedition. They tried to make it clear that they were not subversives. (See Phil. 3:20; John 18:33-38; 1 Peter 2:13-17.) Despite the risk, however, they dared to make their bold and sweeping claim. (See Phil. 2:5-11.)

The proclamation of Jesus' lordship was a sweeping assertation of the crucified and risen Lord's supreme authority over the believer, the church, all worldly authority, the universe, and even death itself.

31

The affirmations of faith in the early church are well summarized in Peter's assertion on the day of Pentecost:

> Let all the house of Israel therefore know assuredly
> that God has made him both Lord and Christ,
> this Jesus whom you crucified.
> —Acts 2:36.

Reflecting on Our Confession

It is one thing to understand clearly the biblical witness in regard to Jesus. It is another thing to work out the meaning of that witness in our thinking and practice. We need to reflect on what we mean when we affirm our faith in Jesus in light of the claims which the church has made about him.

Beginning in the second century of the Christian era, the church became involved in a heated debate about the nature of Christ. This topic posed a perplexing intellectual problem. Was Jesus human, or divine? Or was he both? If he was both, how were the human and divine natures related? These were questions with which learned scholars struggled, trying to fit Christ into the categories of Greek philosophy.

In A.D. 325, the Emperor Constantine summoned the Christian bishops from all over the world to the Council of Nicea to resolve this matter. Seeking to prevent a division in the church, the council attempted to formulate a creedal statement acceptable to all Christians. The statement which they issued, the Nicene Creed, was couched in a language far more technical than the simple affirmations about Jesus in the New Testament. This was their statement:

> We believe . . . in our one Lord Jesus Christ the Son of God, the only-begotten born of the Father, that is of the substance of the Father, God of God, light of light, true God of true God, born, not made, of one substance with the Father . . . , by whom all things were made, which are in heaven and on earth, who for our salvation came down, and became incarnate and was made man, and suffered, and arose again on the third day, and ascended into heaven, and will come to judge the living and the dead.

This declaration failed to solve the problem in the church, for new arguments arose. Different factions tried their hands at defining the precise nature of the God-Man. New councils met and issued creedal statements, many of them quite elaborate. Persons who could not accept these creeds were excommunicated as heretics.

A new assumption had taken over in the church. In regard to any question having to do with our salvation, an authoritative statement of doctrine was necessary. Saving faith required assent to a precise form of words, and the creeds grew ever more elaborate. Some of the Reformation churches wrote confessions of faith which ran for scores of pages.

It was this practice of requiring persons to subscribe to a specific creedal statement to be accepted as a member of the church that led the Disciples pioneers to reject the use of any creed as a test of Christian fellowship. Barton W. Stone and Thomas Campbell both were accused of departing from the Westminster Confession, the doctrinal standard of the Presbyterian churches. Each insisted on following the plain words of scripture alone. Stone, at his ordination to the ministry, made this point clear. When the examining officer asked him if he endorsed the doctrine set forth in the Westminster Confession, he replied, "I do, as far as I see it consistent with the word of God."

Our Disciples founders believed that the creeds had replaced the simple assurance of biblical faith with complicated and abstract language detrimental to sound religion. Most people, they contended, could not understand the issues under debate; and even if they could, the argument had no essential bearing on salvation and the Christian life.

What the Disciples pioneers advocated was a return to the scriptures which they believed contain "all things essential" to our salvation. This plea for simplicity, however, resulted at times in an evasion of theological responsibility. Given the intellectual assumptions which are taken for granted in our time, how are we to understand the words of the Bible?

As we reflect on our own confession, it may help us to examine the thought of Disciples of Christ in regard to Jesus.

Disciples Thinking About Jesus

For a long time the Disciples preaching and teaching about Jesus was determinedly biblical. Alexander Campbell and Walter Scott made much of the scriptural titles, especially Messiah. They referred to Christ as Lawgiver and King, and spoke constantly of his authority. Others emphasized terms such as Ruler, Judge, High Priest, and Lamb of God. No biblical title, however, was applied to him more frequently than Son of God. Even this term carried unmistakable overtones of divine authority.

Late in the nineteenth century, a noticeable change came over Disciples' thinking and preaching. The new biblical scholarship helped us to see that the books of the New Testament are products of particular historical situations. We could discern more clearly what Jesus had meant to persons in those circumstances. But we also realized more keenly the difference between those circumstances and our own. Becoming more conditioned to living in a democratic society, people grew restive under the old restraints of authoritarian religion.

Consequently, we began to think of Jesus more in human terms. We referred to him simply as Jesus, the Nazarene, or the Galilean. He was the Son of Man, the Friend of sinners, the Master, the Great Teacher. Interest centered more on the quality of his human life, the insights of his teachings, and the goodness and joy he inspires in us. Still more recently, we have spoken of Jesus as "the Man for Others," "the New Being," the One truly free, and the Liberator. More and more, we have emphasized his humanity. Some have even minimized the titles of deity as belonging to an earlier age.

Nevertheless, Disciples are still deeply involved with the person of Jesus. We still study the New Testament and ponder deeply its witness to the meaning of his life. Yet we admit that different aspects of that witness speak more compellingly to us now than earlier. Possibly we are too timid today about attributing to Jesus the full majesty of some of the great names which the Gospels and epistles bestow upon him. Yet almost any new emphasis picks up some important aspect of his character and ministry which others have overlooked.

In pondering the faith we proclaim about Jesus, we need to listen to one another, and to other Christians, for a witness to elements in the understanding of Jesus which we have missed. It is important that we continue our careful study of the scriptures for their testimony to the meaning he may have for our lives and for the whole world. It is supremely important to remember that we are united with one another not by our explanations of Jesus, but by the Person who has inspired all of the various doctrines in regard to him.

For faith in Jesus Christ is a personal faith. That is, it centers in a person, not in a set of doctrines. And it involves us believers in the totality of our being. The meaning of Christ is a relationship into which we are drawn. It is best expressed in those New Testament confessions addressed directly to Jesus: "You are the Christ" and "My Lord and my God."

It was this personal aspect of faith that Disciples sought to emphasize by the slogan "No creed but Christ." By going back before the church had begun to formulate elaborate doctrinal statements, they were shifting the focus from propositions to a Person. Alexander Campbell insisted that faith in Jesus as the Christ, and obedience to him as Lord, should constitute "the only test of Christian character" and "the only bond of Christian union."

In recent years, however, most of us have come to see certain legitimate uses for affirmations of belief. Summaries of the common faith serve for instruction and for unison testimony in worship. Increasing numbers of congregations now use such declarations on occasion. Perhaps most widely used today is the covenantal statement (paragraph 1) in the Preamble to *The Design for the Christian Church (Disciples of Christ)*. This affirmation, printed at the beginning of this book, also appears as No. 490 in the *Hymnbook for Christian Worship*.

The Great Commitment

For each of us the Christian life begins with the Good Confession of faith in Jesus as the Christ. Lin D. Cartwright, a prominent Disciples minister, has called this confession "the Great Commitment." When we affirm that for us Jesus is Christ and Lord, we are committing our lives to the service of God whom he reveals to us. This means that we give him first place in our loyalty because he represents the best and the highest we know.

If we were asked to describe what Jesus means to us individually, we would probably use different words and even different concepts. But the Christian Church does not examine us on our understanding to see if it conforms to someone else's doctrine, or any official statement of faith. The one thing the congregation wants to be sure of, when we make our confession, is that with total seriousness we give Jesus Christ the supreme place in our lives. The real issue is loyalty.

Jesus Christ our Lord then sets us free. The greater our commitment to him, the more completely we are freed from our lower selves, from our sin and guilt and fear, from our preoccupation with false values. Responding to him as Lord frees us to our better selves, to love of neighbor, to the realization of God's purpose for our lives.

Day by day, through all the passing years, we find the beloved figure of Jesus out ahead of us, calling us on to further achievement, inspiring us to a better life than we yet have known, imparting to us his joy. At the end of life, whenever it comes, we expect him to be waiting out beyond us, saying, "Because I live, you shall live also."

The freedom and loyalty which spring from the great commitment make possible the common life which Christians share in the church. Because we have bound our hearts to Christ, we are bound to one another. The church is one because of the common loyalty we have all pledged to Christ.

Moreover, confessing Jesus as Christ and Lord has radical and transforming implications for the life of the world. The book of Acts presents a missionary strategy for carrying the gospel to the centers of power and culture. Across the centuries the church has undertaken to establish a Christian society and a Christian culture. Although the Christian forces in our own time make up only a minority of the world's population, the church still pursues this vision and seeks to give voice in the political arena to ideals of integrity, justice, and compassion.

Meanwhile, we Disciples continue to "confess that Jesus is the Christ, the Son of the living God, and proclaim him Lord and Savior of the world." In making the great commitment, we work to transform our lives, the lives of others, and our culture as a whole, by bringing them into closer accord with the will of Christ.

For Reflection and Discussion

Test your memory of what Disciples affirm about Jesus by filling in the missing words in the following sentence:
"We confess that Jesus _IS_ _THE_ _CHRIST_, _THE_ _SON_ _OF_ _THE_ _LIVING_ _GOD_,
And proclaim him _LORD_ _AND_ _SAVIOR_ _OF_ _THE_ _WORLD_."
What meanings are conveyed by the words *confess* and *proclaim* in this affirmation?

If a complete concordance of the Bible is available, look up the words *Savior, Christ,* and *Lord.* Count the number of times each of these words is used as a title for Jesus in the New Testament. Which of these titles do you find most helpful for expressing what Jesus means to you?

What reasons would you have for agreeing—or disagreeing—with the author's views in regard to the use of the statement "I take him [Jesus] as my personal Savior" in the confessional formula? How would you describe the saving work of Christ?

Review briefly what is said in this chapter about the meanings conveyed by the titles *Christ* and *Lord* in the earliest confessions of faith. What, precisely, does each of these titles signify to you as a twentieth-century Christian?

In the light of what is said in this chapter about the personal commitment implied by confessing that Jesus is Christ and Lord, what is your understanding of what this confession requires of you?

What suggestions would you have for working to bring our common life into closer accord with the will of God revealed in Jesus Christ?

Disciples of Christ, as the author reminds us, have responded to sectarian doctrines about Jesus as a test of fellowship by advocating the slogan "No Creed but Christ." What meaning does this slogan convey to you? How adequately does it express your personal convictions about the basis for membership in the church?

What are your personal feelings about the use of a formal affirmation of faith as a part of the order of worship in the church? What reasons would you have for using—or not using—the Affirmation of Faith in the Preamble to *The Design for the Christian Church (Disciples of Christ)?*

We rejoice in God,
    maker of heaven and earth. . . .
In the communion of the Holy Spirit
    we are joined together in discipleship.

3

WE REJOICE IN GOD

Biblical Faith and the Gospel of Grace

To CONFESS Jesus as Christ and Lord implies a great deal about God. In the mounting conviction of his disciples, Jesus had come to do God's supreme work. He stood in a unique relationship to God; indeed, he was God's Messiah, God's Son, God's supreme Servant. The disciples, in their experience of Jesus, had been dealing with God more intimately and directly than any human beings had ever done before. They had seen "the light of the knowledge of the glory of God in the face of Christ" (2 Cor. 4:6).

In this chapter we focus primarily on the nature of God as understood in the light of Jesus Christ. Yet we cannot talk about God without talking about ourselves and all other human beings. Strange as it may seem, in view of some notions of divine majesty, Jesus made clear that God's supreme involvement with the life of earth is with persons.

How then shall we think about God's relation to humanity? What have been the particular interests of Disciples of Christ as they have witnessed to faith in God?

The Gospel of God

We need to recognize, first of all, the surprising degree to which our thinking about God is influenced by factors other than the Bible. Indeed, we tend to work with axioms foreign to the language of biblical faith. Yet we scarcely notice this fact. Our theological discussions, and much of the popular talk about God, reflect premises of classical philosophy. We begin with our presuppositions and fail to see the quite different assumptions of the biblical writers.

God in the Western Mind

It seems natural to us to think of God first of all as Creator. Does not the Bible start with Genesis, giving us in this book of beginnings two ancient stories of creation? When our children ask, "Who made that?" we answer, "God." The more we learn of the universe, the more we are struck with awe at its marvels. Moreover, some of the most reverent people in the world are also scientists.

In the historic creeds of the church, Christians for centuries have designated God as "maker of heaven and earth." Disciples also include this same ascription to God in our affirmation of faith. Our sense of the power of God derives, in no small part, from experience of overwhelming natural forces, such as wind and wave, earthquake and fire.

From the creativity of God we move to the divine character. God is "the high and lofty One who inhabits eternity, whose name is Holy" (Isa. 57:15). Because God is like that, human beings are expected to keep the divine commandments. Most high religions, and certainly the biblical faith, inculate upright behavior as our duty toward God. Primitive religion interpreted sickness and disaster as judgments or marks of divine displeasure. Even today, despite the protest of Job or the agony of Jesus on the cross, some Christians believe that much human suffering is heavenly retribution for some particular sin.

After we have probed the creativity of God and talked about God's righteousness, then we speak of God's love—especially as it is made known to us in the words and life of Jesus. Beginning to think biblically now, we reflect on God's concern for the smallest details of our lives. We see God calling us toward greater fulfillment of the

40

It seems natural to us to think of God first of all as Creator. . . . Israel spoke of God . . . as the living One who met them in the crises of their corporate life.

Religious News Service Photo.

possibilities within us, as meeting us with care and strength in critical moments of our lives.

Christians see such divine and personal love as more than simply an attribute of God. It is God's essential character. "For God is love" (1 John 4:8).

Alexander Campbell sometimes spoke of God in language that was more philosophical than biblical. He, too, used the titles of Creator, Lawgiver, and Redeemer to describe the divine attributes. As Creator, God is revealed most conspicuously as "wisdom, power, and goodness"; as Lawgiver, "justice, truth, and holiness"; and as Redeemer, "mercy, condescension, and love." In each of these manifestations, God is "infinite, immutable, and eternal." For all his good intentions, Campbell's thinking about God betrays the habits of a Western mind.

Many of us, no doubt, tend to fall into this same trap. We have become so accustomed to thinking of God in arguments or rational proofs, listing a series of concepts in systematic order. Let us consider now the mode of thought in which the Bible speaks of Yahweh.

God in Biblical Faith

The faith of the people called Israel begins not with the creation, but with the Exodus. It derives not from wondering about the origin of the universe, but from the deliverance of this people from slavery in Egypt. Also, it came about through God's initiative. God came to this people under the name of Yahweh, meaning the One who is ever with you and ever out ahead of you. (This conception of Yahweh as an eternal presence seems closer to the meaning of the Hebrew term than the conventional translation, "I AM WHO I AM," in Exod. 3:14.)

It was Yahweh who called to the fugitive Moses from a burning bush and sent him back to Egypt. It was Yahweh, speaking through the halting tongue of Moses, who projected the ideal of freedom into the hearts of the oppressed. It was Yahweh who made Moses' words of liberation credible to slaves so crushed by their burdens that they had ceased to believe in freedom and could only cry out in misery.

It was Yahweh, the Israelites believed, who sent upon Egypt the succession of disasters that left Pharaoh no option but to let them go. It was Yahweh who opened a safe passage through the sea for the escaping slaves and who destroyed the military might of the oppressor for venturing into the path which God had opened up for the oppressed.

Israel spoke of God, therefore, not as an abstract notion, but as the living One who met them in the crises of their corporate life. At Sinai, through Moses, Yahweh made a covenant with Israel, giving them the divine commandments (Exod. 20). Later, under Joshua, they took possession of the land of Canaan, regarding it as Yahweh's gift. Here they dwelt, governed by a succession of leaders whom they believed Yahweh had chosen for them.

As the great military empires of Egypt, Assyria, and Babylonia trampled over Israel and Judah, the prophets announced these disasters as Yahweh's judgments on a disobedient people. In a time of utter despair, a great prophet of the Exile began to speak of another exodus. Yahweh was about to do a new thing for his people. He was going to bring the exiles back to their homeland, virtually recreating a people out of nothing (Isa. 43:48). Many of them eventually made the long trek back to rebuild their homes and the temple.

During and after the Exile, scribes gathered the traditions, laws, and scattered writings of Israel into the book which became their sacred scripture, and which Christians call the Old Testament. Throughout the Hebrew Bible, God is the Holy One who confronts the chosen people in one situation after another, in the entire story of their national life. Yahweh is the ever-present Reality with whom they have to deal, in every moral choice they face. To the Israelites, Yahweh was more than an abstract explanation of how everything began; only later did they tell their stories of creation.

Central to their faith was the ever-present One who constantly reminded them:

> "I am the LORD [Yahweh] your God,
>   who brought you out of the land of Egypt,
>   out of the house of bondage.
> You shall have no other gods before me.
> You shall not . . ."
>   —Exodus 20:2-4.

To Jesus, a true child of Israel, God was also the supreme Reality, both in present experience and in the imminent future. According to the Gospel of Mark, Jesus came preaching God's message of a radical ethical demand:

> "The time has come, and the reign of God is near;
>   repent, and believe this good news."
>   —Mark 1:15 (Goodspeed).

His preaching demanded a righteousness of the entire being, not just of conformity to a set of rules (Matt. 5:17—6:18). He taught that God waited with eager readiness to begin the divine reign at any moment.

To the poor and oppressed, and to the poor in spirit, to all who penitently opened their lives to God's will, the reign would come as a gift of grace. It would completely overturn the injustices of the present age. On the impenitent, especially the rich and proud who relied on their positions of power, God's reign would come as judgment. In which of these categories do you think most of us today would fit?

Jesus anticipated the new age with eagerness and joy, for it would bring God's blessings to everyone who would repent and accept God's forgiveness. He taught his disciples to pray earnestly:

> Your name be held in reverence,
> Your reign appear,
> Your will be done,
>   On earth as in heaven.
>   —Matthew 6:9-10 (free translation).

Like his Israelite ancestors, Jesus saw God at work in the world, generously bestowing gifts on all kinds of people. God gives these gifts out of an overflowing love for all, not because anyone deserves them, but because we are all God's children. God makes the sun to shine on the good and the evil, and the rain to fall on the just and the unjust. God clothes the wild flowers in incomparable beauty, feeds the birds, and provides for human needs. As for natural disasters, Jesus saw them happening to both the wise and the foolish.

Moreover, accidents and human cruelty bring suffering and death to their victims without distinguishing the righteous from the sinners. As the apostles later would phrase it, God is no respecter of persons. Yet God takes note even of a sparrow's fall. God's greatest longing is for sinners to repent and enter into the joy of the divine reign. It is urgent that they act before the consequences of their folly and sin bring down destruction upon them as God puts the old age to an end and makes all things new.

More than anyone before him, Jesus taught of God's love for every person. In his own speaking to God, he used the Aramaic word *Abba,* an incredibly endearing and intimate term. Our English versions translate *Abba* with our word Father, as in Luke 11:2. Mark records that Jesus, when he was praying in Gethsemane, addressed God as "Abba, Father" (Mark 14:36). What is so incredible about this is that *Abba* is really more accurately translated "Daddy" or "Papa." It is the word which a tiny child first babbles for a loving parent.

Few of us could bring ourselves to pray, "Our Papa (or Our Daddy) who art in heaven." Yet this is precisely the word which Jesus habitually used for God. It became so firmly fixed in the minds of the disciples that they too taught others to pray in the same manner. Even in mission churches where people did not speak the language of Jesus, Christians learned to pray, "Abba" (Rom. 8:15; Gal. 4:6).

No one before Jesus had ever dared to speak of God in such an intimate way. In a few instances in the Old Testament God had been likened to a mother or a father, but never Papa! Jesus taught that God is as near, as loving, as constantly present, and as desperately needed by all of us as is a human parent by a tiny child. He could speak of God with reverent awe, as in Matthew 6:9 or Mark 10:18, yet also with a child-like trust.

God in Modern Usage

Today we have problems with Jesus' name for God. It may not say to many persons precisely what he had in mind.

For one thing, when *Abba* was translated it came out as Father, a term different in tone and even in meaning. Then, as philosophical ideas about God began to take over Christian thought, Father became "the third person of the trinity." In the Middle Ages, "God the Father" named the austere Ruler and Judge of all humanity, and Jesus' accent was only dimly remembered, if at all. With this heritage, few persons today who sing the Doxology or the Gloria Patri would imagine, from hearing them, the Papa-God of whom Jesus spoke so simply and endearingly.

More recently another problem has surfaced for us. The movement for the liberation and equality of women has made us aware of the oppressiveness of language, even when the speaker may intend no offense. The use in English of masculine words to denote the common gender resulted in saying "man" or "mankind" to designate "humanity," "all men" to mean "all people," or "he" to substitute for a common noun like "person" or "Christian." To quote an old biblical saying like "He who has ears to hear, let him hear" is to risk making half the human race feel left out.

Persons sensitized to this issue have begun to find ways of avoiding the offensive practice. Some leaders of worship take pains to alter the words of hymns, even the scriptures, which use such long accepted forms. Much of the sexist language in the Bible comes from the translators; yet much of it also is in the original text. Especially is this true of the masculine titles for God.

Thoughtful Christians do not imagine that God is really male—or female. These categories simply do not apply to God. Yet many traditional names for deity are masculine in form: King, Lord, and especially Father. Also they are commonly followed by the pronoun "he." But if we do not use the familiar biblical titles, how then do we speak of God as personal?

We may avoid, insofar as possible, the use of the pronoun "he" and of masculine names. Instead of "King" we may say "Sovereign," instead of "kingdom," say "reign" (actually a better translation of the term Jesus used). Or we may address God in terms which do not imply gender, such as Spirit, Creator, Friend, or God of love. Yet none of these carries the intimate, personal associations of Father—much less of Jesus' beloved name for God, *Abba* (Papa).

Parent is not a term of familiar address. A few persons speak of God alternately as "she" and "he," which is at best confusing. Some address prayers to "Our Mother who art in heaven," but this presents problems for many persons. Moreover, it breaks a tradition of twenty centuries in using the distinctive Christian name for God the Father, even if "Father" communicates only partially the force of Jesus' *"Abba!"*

Whatever solution we may ultimately reach in regard to the problem of sexism in language, and it cannot be ignored, we must keep in mind the main point about biblical faith in God. It is not a matter of setting out a series of abstract assertions about the divine nature. Rather biblical faith speaks of God as the righteous and holy One, before whom we live out our lives in faithfulness or unfaithfulness. In the highest reach of all, Jesus talks of God as the One to whom we may turn with the implicit faith of a little child surrounded by a parent's unfailing love.

Saving Acts of God

In the story told in the New Testament, Jesus' teaching about God remains entirely free of sentimentality, as does the gospel afterwards preached by the church. The love which God offers us, in spite of human sin, lessens in no way the abhorrence with which God views that sin within us. The righteousness of God necessarily acts to condemn human wickedness totally. Jesus saw that condemnation as ready to break out upon the earth in imminent judgment.

Nevertheless, Jesus took no delight, as some believers seem to do, in the thought that the wicked would get "what is coming to them."

Rather he saw God as longing for signs of repentance and more than ready to forgive everyone who will turn from sin (Luke 15:20). But even God can extend forgiveness only to those who inwardly long to receive it, and who are willing to accept with that forgiveness a total redirection of their lives. With the coming of God's reign, everyone and everything on earth will voluntarily bring their desires into harmony with the holy will of God.

The Gospel That Saves

Meanwhile, Jesus is under no illusions about the seriousness of the human situation. He finds it easy to think of prostitutes and others who are tagged as sinners entering the reign of God, for they know their sin. On hearing the gospel, many of them are turning to God in repentance—much more readily than those who exploit and condemn them. With the rest of humanity, especially the respectable members of an unjust society and those who regard themselves as righteous, Jesus has a more serious problem.

It is these "good" people whom Jesus sees as needing to repent even more than tax collectors and sinners (Matt. 21:31). They are hard-hearted, faithless, foolish, and perverse.

Jesus' diagnosis proved to be accurate. It was not the hookers and the winos who sent Jesus to the cross. Rather it was the esteemed members of the establishment. Political authorities, religious leaders, and military officers conspired in this deed. Many of his own disciples forsook him. Only a few women and one or two men whose friendship for Jesus was secret stood by while he died (John 19:25-39) as an innocent victim of the sin from which he had tried in vain to call the very people who had him executed.

From the early Christian preachers we hear much more about the horror of sin than we do from Jesus. Probably this is because the cross had brought it home to them. They had seen what sin in themselves and in others had done to him. Jesus' crucifixion was enough to convict all humanity of sin. The story of the cross continues to convict and move to repentance those who hear.

In the wholly unjustifiable death of Jesus—the one "who knew no sin," crucified on account of the sins of others—the early Christians saw the world's most powerful witness to the redemptive love of God. In this event God was revealed as suffering whenever the helpless and despised are made to suffer. God was made known as fully sharing in the agony and disgrace of the outcast in order to help persons see their sinfulness in exploiting others. And through the cross, the readiness of God to forgive had been made compellingly clear.

The disciples believed that in raising Jesus from the dead God had made him both Lord and Christ. Thus they called on all who would listen to repent, to be baptized, to receive God's forgiveness, and to enter newness of life. After the crucifixion and resurrection, the gospel Jesus had preached became, on the lips of his disciples, the gospel about Jesus. The emphasis shifted from the imminence of God's reign to the Messiahship of Jesus through whom God offered forgiveness of sins.

The apostle Paul, probably more than any other Christian of the first century, gave urgent thought to the human situation which had led to Jesus' crucifixion. He viewed the entire human race as captive to sin, deserving of condemnation, unable by any human power to change that condition, and so under the sentence of death. He drew on the old story of the Fall in the Garden of Eden to explain our predicament. Because Adam and Eve, parents of all human beings, sinned, we all have sinned. Moreover, the wages of sin is death.

Yet Paul's gospel also told of a Second Adam and a new humanity freed from bondage to sin and death. The founder of this new race is, of course, Jesus Christ. Through his death and resurrection, God has broken the powers of sin and death and now offers the power to become new beings. "As in Adam all die," said Paul, "so also in Christ shall all be made alive" (1 Cor. 15:22).

Notions of Original Sin

Generations of theologians who came after Paul made his imagery central to their understanding of the gospel. Some of his ideas, however, were carried to such an extreme that the early Disciples leaders rejected many of the prevailing doctrines in their time as unbiblical. To understand certain basic beliefs of the Disciples of Christ we need to examine some notions widely held in the nineteenth century. Not all of these have been totally abandoned even today.

The idea of "original sin" was elaborated in the theology of John Calvin (1509-1564). Like St. Augustine before him, Calvin understood Paul to mean that Adam's fall had so corrupted human nature that every person born into the world carried the divine sentence of condemnation. For this reason, Augustine had urged the baptism of infants, so that the saving grace of Christ might be bestowed sacramentally to save them from eternal hell. This belief in the damnation of unbaptized infants was widely accepted on the American frontier, and some people still believe it. However, few

Protestant communions which practice infant baptism today base their practice on the doctrine of original sin.

The strict Calvinists of the early nineteenth century insisted on an equally troubling doctrine, that of double predestination. Like Paul and Augustine, Calvin believed that those who are saved have been chosen by God for inclusion among the elect "from before the foundation of the world." So also with "the lost." Even before creation, they have been "reprobated" or doomed to eternal damnation. Not even baptism can save those whom God has not chosen. Double predestination means both the election of some and the reprobation of many.

Since all were considered deserving of eternal punishment, Calvinists spoke of the "mystery" of grace. God had, after all, chosen some to be saved, even though no one had a right to eternal blessedness. But those who were "lost" could do nothing about it. Not even prayer could change the divine will. The elect must await the overpowering inward event which signified that they had been singled out for salvation.

It was at this point that the Disciples pioneers reacted most strongly to Calvinism. Although Alexander Campbell believed that human nature had been contaminated by Adam's sin, he and the other Disciples leaders could not accept the idea of an elect few. They urged that every sinner is capable of hearing the gospel, believing it, and turning to Christ in repentance. Everyone who claims the promise of grace by being baptized, they insisted, has divine assurance of eternal life. Moreover, infants, who share in humanity's fallen nature, are considered innocent until they reach the age of accountability.

In most of the churches today thinking about election and reprobation has undergone a vast change. But the preaching of the early Disciples came as good news to many people. Imagine what this message of grace meant to distraught souls, troubled by the burden of sin and guilt, in a time when most Christians believed in a literal hellfire for the wicked.

In more recent years, a theological movement popularly called neo-orthodoxy has taken another look at the biblical doctrines of sin and salvation. Four of its emphases have been rather widely accepted among Disciples of Christ.

• *A new seriousness about sin.* Despite our sentimental self-esteem, human nature is seriously flawed by its innate tendency to self-love. We pursue our own interests at the expense of others. We do

49

not love our neighbors as we love ourselves. We strive more for preference than for justice. Self-seeking of individuals becomes exaggerated on the part of the human groups in which we participate. Our self-love mars all of our relationships. This the neo-orthodox theologians termed as original sin.

We cannot will our way or earn our way out of this predicament. Rather in faith we cast ourselves on the grace of God, and God grants forgiveness. By giving ourselves, in the spirit of Christ, to the struggle for justice we express the love for neighbor.

• *A dynamic understanding of reprobation and grace.* In the old Calvinistic doctrine which divided humanity between "us" and "them," there were only a few of us (those elected for salvation) and many of them (those reprobated for damnation). Karl Barth and Reinhold Niebuhr, two great theologians, helped Christians to see the judgment of the cross on every person. God's reprobation and God's grace are directed concurrently on each one of us. All of us need to confess our sin before God. Yet at the same instant that God repudiates us because of our sin, God holds us in the grace of Christ and receives us as though we were righteous.

This doctrine requires us—every person—constantly to search our own motives and to cast ourselves in utter trust on divine grace.

• *The universality of Christ's saving acts.* The old understanding of election tended to limit the work of God in Christ to a relatively few people, the "elect." But just as the cross shatters our pretensions as individuals, so it does corporately as well. God established the unity of humankind in creation. So likewise in redemption, when "the Word became flesh" (John 1:14), that act of incarnation identified God with all humanity, the whole human race. On the cross, Christ "died for all" (2 Cor. 5:15). By the grace of God all have been forgiven.

The thinking of some New Testament writers seemed to be moving toward the realization that, as far as God is concerned, the whole universe has been redeemed. This is close to Jesus' perception that God is ready to give the reign of heaven wherever hearts are open in penitence and receptivity. The Book of Revelation, while it depicts in vivid imagery the overthrow of the wicked, also invites us to contemplate the universal import of the eternal victory of Christ.

• *Election to special service.* The Israelites, looking back to the call of Abraham and Sarah, saw themselves as God's chosen people. Sometimes this sense of election prompted a disdain and cruelty toward other people. In taking up this idea of election from the Bible, Christians also often fell into the same trap.

As the Hebrew prophets discerned, God's election of a people is for the purpose of performing a mission, not an act of special favor. As in the case of Jesus, that mission often necessitates self-sacrifice. Biblical election is not a matter of setting "us" against "them," but of calling us to give ourselves for them.

Disciples of Christ have not been enthusiastic about all aspects of neo-orthodox doctrine. Nevertheless, we tended to pick up these four emphases which grow out of deep reflection on the witness of the Bible and the long Christian tradition.

Other Issues Concerning God

It would be impossible, in one chapter, to deal with all the important questions about God. Here we have focused primarily on the gospel of God. But it may be helpful to suggest very briefly some topics to which Disciples have given particular attention.

Most of the churches which came out of the Protestant Reformation have emphasized the work of God through Christ in redemption. The weight of concern has come down on sin, judgment, and forgiveness. The classical liturgies begin with public confession of sin and a declaration of absolution. The less formal, even folksy, tradition of revivalism has made the same emphasis.

But Disciples have not consistently followed this pattern in worship. Without denying the reality of sin, they have usually given more attention to other aspects of the human condition which also indicate the need for God. Often Disciples worship centers on one or more of these rather than always focusing on sin.

We have been more inclined to reflect on our creaturehood in the good world God created, and offer to God our praise, love, and trust. Mindful of human ignorance and superstition, we rejoice in the illumination we receive through the church and "the light of scripture." Sometimes in worship we simply rejoice in the Lord, in the goodness made known through God's word and God's world. In any case, our worship is not always marked by a heavy emphasis on sin.

Some religious groups have emphasized the work of the Holy Spirit in conversion to soften hard hearts and move sinners to a saving faith. When the great religious excitement of the revival broke out in "spiritual exercises' at Cane Ridge, Kentucky, in 1801, Barton W. Stone interpreted them as signs of God's work. Yet he insisted that such behavior was not necessary to conversion. Disciples generally regard it as of little religious consequence, perhaps even harmful.

51

In thinking about the Holy Spirit, Disciples usually refer to the second chapter of Acts. Here the emphasis is on the gift of the Spirit to the community of believers, the preaching of the gospel concerning Jesus Christ, and the promise of the Spirit to those who repented and were baptized. Disciples have regarded the guidance of the Spirit as given primarily through holy scripture and the common mind of the church.

In conversion, Disciples have said, the Spirit operates through the preaching of the gospel to enable the hearers to believe. A majority of them have taken a dubious attitude toward speaking in tongues and other practices of the so-called charismatic movement. They do not prize religious excitement or emotionalism, but rather emphasize the reasonableness of Christian faith.

In reading the New Testament, Disciples have noted that the early Christian experience of God led them to speak of the Father, as Jesus taught them to do, of Jesus Christ the Son of God, and of the Spirit of God which had been given to the church. In a few instances all three are named in one passage (Matt. 28:19; Rom. 1:2-4; 1 Cor. 2:10-16; 2 Cor. 13:13; Eph. 4:3-6). Later the church, trying to reconcile this way of talking with the idea of one God, struggled to formulate a doctrine of the Trinity.

The Disciples regarded themselves as neither trinitarian nor unitarian. Alexander Campbell would not use the term trinitarian because it did not appear in scripture. He even changed one line in the great trinitarian hymn, "Holy, Holy, Holy," so that instead of saying, "God in three Persons, blessed Trinity," people would sing, "God over all, and blest eternally." The ultimate response to the God of the Bible, Disciples believed, is not an argument but a life, as the community of believers seek to live out the common faith in praise and service to God.

In the stained glass window of the old Commencement Hall at Bethany College (Bethany, West Virginia), scene of so many hopes and triumphs, a paraphrase of Romans 9:5 testifies to the faith which sustains all our thought and all our labor:
"God Over All, Blessed For Ever"

The affirmation of faith in the Preamble to *The Design for the Christian Church (Disciples of Christ)* affirms the same note of praise in the sweeping doxology:

> Blessing, glory and honor
> be to God forever. Amen

For Reflection and Discussion

God is identified in the Bible by a variety of titles which express different attributes of the divine character and different perceptions of God's relationship to us. How many of these titles can you recall from memory?

Read and think about these four passages: Genesis 14:19, Exodus 3:6, Deuteronomy 1:30, and Romans 15:6. What insights do these passages offer in regard to the character of God?

Reflect on the affirmation of faith expressed in the Twenty-third Psalm. How would you compare the psalmist's perception of God as "my shepherd" with Jesus' intimate relationship to God as reflected in his use of the Aramaic term *Abba?*

Of the various titles for God mentioned in the Bible which ones do you find most meaningful for describing your personal understanding of God? Which ones do you regard as most appropriate for addressing God in prayer?

What do you understand to be the meaning of the theological phrase "original sin"? How adequately does this phrase express your own understanding of the human condition which hinders us from fulfilling God's purpose for our lives?

How would you interpret what it means to be saved? What do you understand to be the conditions on which God forgives us and reconciles us through fellowship in the community of faith?

What do you understand to be the Disciples thinking in regard to the work of the Holy Spirit? How would you describe the role of the Spirit in your own life?

Biblical scholars sometimes refer to the Bible as the story of God's "mighty acts" in human affairs. How would you describe God's present activity in the world?

We rejoice in . . . the covenant of love
which binds us to God and one another.
Through baptism into Christ
we . . . are made one with the whole
people of God. . . .
At the table of the Lord
we celebrate with thanksgiving
the saving acts and presence of Christ.

4

BOUND TO GOD
AND ONE ANOTHER

Church, Covenant,
Baptism, Communion

THOSE who respond to the gospel of God, by confessing faith in
Jesus Christ the Lord, God gathers together in a joyful company of
believers. In this chapter we focus on the community of Christians
and the quality of the life we share together. First we shall look briefly
at three familiar words which suggest a title for church: covenant-
sacrament-community. In this hyphenated term, each word describes
what is to follow. After a quick glance at each of them we shall
examine the three parts in greater depth.

The final word of this hyphenated title is *community*. As Christians
we belong to a company of disciples. Together we name ourselves a
church, but it is a church still unfulfilled. God calls us to build up the
faith and devotion of this community, to shape forms suitable for its
mission, and to give expression in its common life to the gospel we
profess.

God also calls us to the work of reconciliation, to "bridge the human rift." That means first of all in our own churchly life. Many magnificent building projects demand first some razing of old structures. The great book on the building up of the church begins with a drama of demolition.

The letter to the Ephesians looks at a stubborn barrier in the first-century church—the ugly partition between Jews and Gentiles—then it proclaims, "Christ . . . has made us both one, and has broken down the dividing wall of hostility." He has reconciled "us both in one body through the cross" (Eph. 2:14-16).

The alienations of a hostile society no longer hold within the church. For here Christ has made peace. Thus, as the Second Vatican Council stated in the 1960s, the church has become "a kind of sign" announcing hope to the world. God's intention for a reconciled humanity has already come to fulfillment here. Does the community we are describing sound as if it could be your congregation?

This community is entrusted with a gospel and a vision which can transform human culture. In the hymn, "We Would Be Building," we pray:

> Master, lend us sight
> To see the towers gleaming in the light.

Think about what the great church towers have meant in the inspiration and transformation of cultures. Think of the Cathedral of Holy Wisdom in Constantinople, of Notre Dame in Paris, of Canterbury in London, of the painted white belfry of a humble wooden church in a prairie village.

The towers are not all architectural. Think of Augustine's *City of God,* of Dante's *Divine Comedy,* of Milton's *Paradise Lost* and *Paradise Regained.* Think of musical towers: Bach's *St. Matthew's Passion,* or Handel's *Messiah.* Think of paintings and sculpture, films and novels, and all other forms of artistic creativity inspired by the gospel. Such towers have made the world a different place in which to live.

Too much discussion about the church has to do with housekeeping and remodeling. We talk too little about a church that attracts creative spirits. The vision of Christ can still inspire new and exciting works of art. Thus the church in the world is a transforming community.

This company to which we belong is a *covenant-community.* God brings it into being as, together with God and with one another, we

56

voluntarily assume a sacred bond.

First, God binds the divine Reality to us, and we bind ourselves, as members and as church, to God—to God's love, God's will, God's mission, God's power. Second, God binds us to one another in sacred community, and in fidelity we seal the bond. Being a disciple is not a private vocation. It is a calling within community. Most of us find that community in a congregation.

Then God binds us to the whole body of Christians, and we make ourselves one with all of them. This relationship comes to expression in community and county-wide gatherings, both denominational and ecumenical. Various regional, national, international bodies enable Christians to demonstrate the unity in the common covenant.

Finally, in making covenant with us, God binds us to all humanity, indeed to the entire world. Jesus lived and died for every human being and for the entire cosmos. The risen Christ is Lord of all. In making covenant we commit ourselves to living out the meaning of his lordship everywhere. When we speak of church, we speak of covenant-community.

Within the community, we make our covenant through *sacraments*. This word has not long been loved by Disciples. Nevertheless, we may find it useful, even if it is not a Bible name for a Bible thing. It expresses the meaning of baptism and communion as acts of covenant-making. In the Roman army, the *sacramentum* was the oath of allegiance sworn by a recruit. We can readily understand why Christians very early would seize on this name for the covenant-acts of the church.

Our early Disciples leaders spoke of baptism and communion as ordinances, actions which the Lord ordained or instituted. Yet we keep them for more profound reasons than that they were commanded. Furthermore, when the New Testament speaks of ordinances it is not talking about baptism and communion. So we have come to settle for sacrament, an oath of allegiance. We think of baptism and communion as covenant-sacraments. The church itself is a covenant-sacrament-community.

Idea of Covenant

Consider our spiritual mother Sarai and father Abram, wandering far from home in response to a divine call. Yahweh made covenant with them, gave them new names, and promised them a child (Gen. 15). Abraham became father of the faithful and Sarah their mother. We their children find ourselves bound to their covenant-God.

Five hundred years later, their descendents were enslaved in Egypt. Delivered by God's servant, Moses, they passed through the wilderness to Sinai where Moses communed with God and received divine commands. Returning from the mountain to the people, he made these commands known to them. Then the people solemnly swore an oath of allegiance.

Moses read the book of the covenant to the people, and again they swore their oath: "All that the LORD has spoken we will do" (Exod. 24:7). Sprinkling them with blood from the sacrifice, Moses said, "Behold the blood of the covenant which the LORD has made with you" (vs. 8). Thus did Moses and the people of Israel make covenant with God. That covenantal act altered their history forever, and our history also.

Covenant became the central focus of Israel's religion. In the land of promise, the people went once a year to the shrine of Yahweh to renew the covenant.

There were times, however, when Israel became unfaithful to God and failed to keep the covenant. Breaking covenant meant, as the prophets saw it, much more than a loss of interest in their religion or neglecting to attend religious ceremonies. It meant sanctioning injustices, oppressing the helpless, and exploiting the poor. Keeping covenant meant maintaining a social order marked by public righteousness and justice in all human relationships.

The prophet Jeremiah envisioned Yahweh as making a new covenant with the people of God. No longer would the law be an external requirement, but rather, said Yahweh:

> "I will put my law within them,
> and I will write it upon their hearts;
> and I will be their God,
> and they shall be my people."
> —Jeremiah 31:33.

It was against this background that Jesus came to his last night on earth with his disciples. As the earliest Christians remembered that last supper in an upper room in Jerusalem, they told how Jesus broke bread and shared the cup with them. He said, "This cup is the new covenant in my blood" (1 Cor. 11:25). The new covenant is given and received in a sacrament.

The idea of covenant, essentially a religious concept, has immeasurably enriched secular life. Christian matrimony is a covenant between a man and a woman, and between the couple and

God. In sacred self-giving, husband and wife are united "till death us do part."

Nations have been established by covenant. This idea inspired the thinking of social theorists about the social contract. The Pilgrims, before landing in New England, drew up and signed the Mayflower Compact. The Declaration of Independence represented the dissolution of an old covenant which bound the people of the thirteen colonies to the English Crown. In establishing the United States of America, they entered into a new political covenant, affirming: "With a firm reliance on the protection of Divine Providence, we mutually pledge to each other our lives, our fortunes, and our sacred honor."

In religion, in marriage, and in the life of a nation, a covenant is a sacred bond sealed with an oath or vow of allegiance. In the community of Christians that pledge is called a sacrament. A Christian swears faithfulness to God. God promises faithfulness to the church. This two-way pledge is seen most clearly in the Christian covenant-sacraments of baptism and communion.

Baptism and Covenant

For the first hundred years of the Disciples movement, baptism was one of the main topics preachers discussed in their sermons. They delighted to tell the story about Alexander Campbell's perplexity after the birth of his first child. Should the little girl be baptized or not? What he was debating with himself was whether or not infant baptism has any sanction in the scriptures.

Going to the Greek New Testament, Campbell studied every passage which refers to baptism. After days of pondering this matter, he reached three conclusions: First, baptism is for responsible believers only, not for infants. Second, baptism means immersion. Third, he himself, though christened in infancy, had not been baptized. So not only did he not baptize his infant daughter, but he and his father and their wives went down to Buffalo Creek to be immersed, with a Baptist preacher officiating.

Eventually, however, Disciples tired of a diet of constant preaching on baptism. People wanted something to build them up as Christians. They wanted to deal with world issues. Many of them found much of the old preaching legalistic and external. It was embarrassing ecumenically.

Even more significant was the change which came about in their thinking. Disciples, in increasing numbers, concluded that, in spite of everything, God has also honored the baptism of Methodists,

Congregationalists, Presbyterians, and Roman Catholics—even if they had received it as infants, and even if it was by sprinkling.

Here and there, congregations began to join God in this matter, in spite of their earlier conclusions drawn from the New Testament. Today the practice of inclusive membership is common. Our General Assembly, in 1975, endorsed the principle of "mutual recognition of members" among the various churches in the Consultation of Church Union.

Baptism, as most Disciples now view it, is an act of covenant-making. It symbolizes a covenant between the new disciple and the living Lord, between the neophyte and the church. This act is rich in meaning.

- Our baptism recalls and imitates the baptism of Jesus in the Jordan River (Matt. 3:13-17). Following him in this manner, we covenant to be his disciples and join him in his desire "to fulfill all righteousness."
- Our baptism dramatizes our personal confession of the faith the church proclaims. It enacts the basic elements of the primitive Christian tradition "that Christ died for our sins, . . . that he was buried, that he was raised on the third day" (1 Cor. 15:3).
- Our baptism performs outwardly what happens inwardly in the new believer. The disciple voluntarily dies to an old life, to everything un-Christlike and unloving within us apart from Christ, and rises to walk with Christ in "newness of life" (Rom. 6:3-4; Col. 3:5-17).
- Our baptism, by its action, suggests that in taking off our old garments to enter this bath we lay aside an old life. In the water we are cleansed of sin and guilt. As we put on a clean white robe, we put on Christ. (See 1 Cor. 6:9-11; Gal. 3:27; Col. 3:1-14.)
- Our baptism is an act of initiation which incorporates us into the church, the body of Christ. The Holy Spirit comes to us within the community of the faithful which the Spirit has created and sustains. Plunged into the life of the church, we make covenant with the great company of Christians in the whole world, and they with us. (See 1 Cor. 12:12-13.)
- Our baptism identifies us with all humanity. As Jesus was made one with all humankind and died on the cross to redeem them all, we also by being made one with him in baptism are made one with all those for whom he died. In baptism we commit ourselves to a life of love and self-giving like that of Jesus. (See 2 Cor. 5:14-15.)

Viewed as an act of covenant-making, baptism becomes a

covenant-sacrament which occurs within a community. Not only is it intensely personal in its assurance to and its claims on the persons being baptized. It is also intensely corporate, binding us into the life of the company of Christians. At the same time it is highly secular. Through our baptism God claims us for life in the world as God would have us live, and for all the people of the world for whom Christ gave all.

In covenant-community we affirm that "through baptism into Christ we enter into newness of life and are made one with the whole people of God."

Communion and Covenant

In baptism we make covenant; in communion we renew covenant week by week. With other members of the Christian community we gather in worship at a family table. Here we recall the words of our Lord at the last supper with his disciples. After offering prayers of thanksgiving, together we break bread and drink from the cup.

This simple action of the church goes by various names. In the New Testament, it is commonly called the Lord's supper, the breaking of bread, or communion. The Greek word for the prayer of thanksgiving at the table is *eucharistein*. From this word we get the English noun, "eucharist," which many Christians use to designate this event. In the Roman Catholic Church, the most common designation is the Mass. Probably the designations most commonly used in the churches today are Holy Communion and the Eucharist.

Ironically, this family meal around the Lord's table has been the center of much controversy among Christians. Beginning in the ancient church, Christians moved to a highly literal understanding of the words, "This is my body" and "This is my blood." In the Middle Ages, they began to speak of transubstantiation, meaning an actual change in the substance of the bread and wine. This led to the doctrine of the Real Presence of Christ in the eucharist. Hence it could be observed properly only when an ordained priest, with power to effect the "miracle of the mass," administered it.

Most Protestant churches adopted a somewhat less miraculous understanding of the Lord's supper. A sizable group, including the Disciples of Christ, emphasized the symbolic function of the bread and cup. They interpreted the Lord's supper largely in terms of remembrance. Yet they viewed it as much more than a symbolic action designed to recall the death of Jesus. Disciples quite commonly think of this action as a communion—a term which refers to a present engagement, not a memory of the past.

61

Disciples of Christ, by consistently celebrating the Lord's supper every Lord's day, have made it a central element in their worship. In this respect we are more like the Orthodox and Catholic churches than like other Protestant bodies. Appropriately, the Christian Church (Disciples of Christ) adopted as its symbol the chalice and cross of St. Andrew (both are depicted on the cover).

Our observance of the Lord's Supper as a covenant-sacrament expresses the fullness of our faith. By sharing at the Lord's table:

- We join in dramatically enacting the decisive event in the faith of the church. Remembrance and hope here unite in present action. We are made aware that "as often as you eat this bread and drink the cup, you proclaim the Lord's death until he comes" (1 Cor. 11:26).

- We affirm the presence of the living Lord in the midst of the church. To reenact—in the company of the faithful—key events, in which the hand of God is visible, is to encounter anew the divine love and power which accomplishes our salvation. (See Luke 24:28-36.)

- We join together as members of God's family about the family table. Eating and drinking together, even in this symbolic way, expresses our oneness in Christ. We share a mutual concern for one another, and we make real the unity of the church (1 Cor. 11:17-22).

- Each of us is granted a time of personal communion with the living Christ. This meeting offers an opportunity for self-examination and confession of our sin, and brings us the assurance of the forgiving Savior. It empowers us for our work in the coming days.

- We affirm the oneness of Jesus Christ and ourselves with all who suffer, especially the oppressed, mistreated, and deprived (Matt. 25:31-46). The words "broken body" and "shed blood" remind us of God's presence as suffering love with all victims of the world's cruelty.

- We assert the secular character of our faith. Faith's most sacred act requires wheat and bread, grapes and a cup, and a company of sinners bringing their lives before the Lord. This act is not an escape from the world, but a joyful affirmation of God's involvement with the world.

- We look forward to the final triumph of Christ as Lord of all creation and as Victor over death. We affirm our oneness with the whole company of the redeemed who at last will feast together in our Lord's presence (Rev. 19:9).

We renew the covenant between ourselves and Jesus Christ (Mark 14:24-25). Here once more we claim his love as the dominant power in our lives, both in the church and in the world. In covenant-community we affirm that "at the table of the Lord we celebrate with thanksgiving the saving acts and presence of Christ."

Church as Covenant Community

As Disciples of Christ, our most intimate experience of church is usually in the local community of believers known as a congregation. Yet most of us probably take the congregation for granted. In many cases, it was here before we were, and we seldom pause to wonder how it got started. If we do, we ask questions about when it was organized, who started it, and where. But a more profound question would be: *How* does a congregation come into being?

This question deeply troubled the English Puritans in the seventeenth century. Many of them demanded reforms in the Church of England that were more rigorous than the reforms achieved by King Henry VIII or Parliament. Due to their convictions, they had come to feel they could no longer in good conscience worship in the established church. Consequently, uncompromising Separatists began to establish new congregations on Puritan lines.

What makes such a congregation a true church when no bishop will certify it or take responsibility for it? You have to depend on the members themselves to make decisions. A shoemaker, a scullery maid, a fishwife, a tinker, a nurse, a butcher, a baker, a candlestick-maker—what qualifies a motley crew like that as a church of Jesus Christ?

It is crucial to note the way in which the Puritans resolved the question of how a congregation becomes a church. They entered into a solemn covenant with one another and with God. They pledged to acknowledge Jesus Christ as their Lord and to walk in his ways. They took the Bible as their rule. Within these sacred commitments, the congregation made all decisions in regard to their Christian witness and life together.

Many congregations of Disciples of Christ came into being in much the same way. There was no one on earth to make their decisions for them. Yet they did not run the show on the basis of popular whim. Rather, all the members together assumed the sacred responsibility of discerning the mind of Christ. They took on the burden of establishing a church in a covenant relationship. Often they drew up a written document to which the charter members all signed their names. By that covenant God made them into a church.

When new members unite with a congregation which is constituted as a covenant community they enter into the covenant. This is the essence of congregational polity. Majority rule is implied by this arrangement, but it is a majority of a particular kind of persons— Christians. They have pledged themselves to Christ and to one another, sworn to conduct their common life as a true church of Christ, and to be guided by the Scriptures.

In this covenant relationship, all members of the congregation are committed to fulfilling their calling as Christians, to support one another, to advance the mission of the church, and to give themselves in and for the world. Made one through covenant-sacrament of baptism, they renew their vows, week by week, in the covenant-sacrament of holy communion.

To speak of our responsibility under the covenant, however, is not to suggest that perfection of the church is attained through human striving. Actually, a covenant is an audacious claim on God's grace and a proclamation of divine faithfulness. The point is that wherever or whenever we respond in sincerity to the will of God, God is there to meet us in our good intentions. In every situation, God stands ready to make up out of divine goodness whatever is lacking in our performance.

God initiates the covenant, and each congregation where faithful disciples undertake to follow Christ is a token of God's grace. In covenant-community the members affirm: "We rejoice in . . . the covenant of love which binds us to God and one another."

Christian Church (Disciples of Christ)

The community of faith is much larger than a single congregation. It includes many local communities of Christians. Every congregation, no matter how strong or how large, needs all the others just as surely as each disciple needs to be bound with other disciples in a congregation.

Alexander Campbell thought of the great church as a "community of communities." He advocated a "general church organization" which would give expression to this thought. But the time was not yet ripe. The frontier folk who made up so many of the congregations of Disciples in the nineteenth century suspected that outsiders did not understand their situation. Some of them recalled unpleasant experiences with churchly authorities. They were suspicious of any

64

organizational structure that might attempt to impose its will on the congregation.

For more than a hundred years, Disciples tried to carry on their common life in the United States and Canada as if there were no church beyond the local congregations. They organized missionary societies, Sunday school associations, and boards for a variety of good causes. They gathered annually in conventions. But all these agencies, they said nervously, were secular corporations organized under civil law. They were not ecclesiastical bodies, not the church.

Through all those years some of the greatest apostles and saints of the movement, its teachers and leaders, had no ministerial titles. They preached, they sacrificed, they prayed, they wore out their lives for the churches—but they were called corresponding secretaries, executive secretaries, and in a few instances, presidents.

What about the work established by missionaries in India and Africa, in Latin America and the Philippines, and other far places of the world? These were missions, not churches, administered by secretaries of the societies.

This kind of pious subterfuge could not be sustained forever. We could not keep on deluding ourselves about what God had really given us, or about the real nature of the church as taught in the New Testament. Then, early in the 1950s, it happened. Disciples began to speak of our life together, in states and provinces, in the United States and Canada, as *church.*

Some groups dared to use titles such as "the Christian Church in Indiana," "the Christian Church in Oklahoma," and "the Christian Church in the United States and Canada." Instead of telling these daring souls they were wrong, we knew deep within ourselves that they were right. We even began to notice phrases in the New Testament which we had overlooked before, such as "the church throughout all Judea and Galilee and Samaria" (Acts 9:31).

The International Convention of Christian Churches (Disciples of Christ) at its Assembly in 1960 authorized the appointment of a Commission on Brotherhood Restructure. This group of 130 Disciples labored at its task for several years. Its members held innumerable dialogues with Disciples in congregations, in districts, in states, and in agency boards. In 1966 the commission submitted a draft of a *Provisional Design* to the International Convention where it was discussed and revised.

The following year this document was sent out to area assemblies and to the agencies for their response. All of the assemblies and agencies, with one exception, approved it. Final approval of the

Provisional Design was given in 1968 at Kansas City by the International Convention, which immediately reconstituted itself as the General Assembly of the Christian Church (Disciples of Christ).

This action took place around the communion table. As representatives of the Disciples of Christ throughout the United States and Canada we were struggling to recognize and express the reality of church. Church, in the biblical sense, is constituted by covenant.

Bound to God and to all God's people in sacred covenant, we can never think of the Christian community as limited to our own particular denomination. By our baptism we are united with the one body; at the table of the Lord we reaffirm our oneness with all who own the lordship of Christ.

The ecumenical movement, to which Disciples are unreservedly committed, is giving increasing attention to the meaning of covenant as the way to Christian union. The issue is not primarily a matter of cleverness in merging church structures, compromise over theological differences, or concern for greater efficiency. The real point is that all Christians and all churches take seriously our involvement with one another because of the covenant we have all made with God, and God with us. In our covenantal relationships we belong to one another. We belong to Jesus Christ as Lord. It is Christ who makes us church, a covenant-sacrament-community.

For Reflection and Discussion

The church is described, in this chapter, as a covenant-sacrament-community. In what ways, if any, does this perception serve to enhance your personal understanding of membership in the church?

What suggestions would you have for improving the quality of life which Christians share together in a congregation that acknowledges the lordship of Jesus Christ?

What is your response to the author's interpretation of baptism and the Lord's supper as covenant-sacraments? To what extent does this way of viewing these acts enhance their meaning for you?

What do you understand to be the distinctive features of a covenant relationship with God and with one another? What opportunities does your congregation offer its members for participating in a covenantal relationship?

What do you perceive to be identifying characteristics of the Christian Church (Disciples of Christ)? In what ways do Disciples seek to manifest a sense of oneness with the whole people of God?

An important function of the church, as described in the New Testament, is to continue Jesus' ministry of reconciliation in the world. In what ways is your congregation seeking to break down barriers to fellowship in "the household of God" (Eph. 2:19)?

In Christ's name and by his grace
  we accept our mission of witness
  and service to all people. . . .
In the communion of the Holy Spirit
  we are joined together in discipleship
  and in obedience to Christ . . . .
Within the universal church
  we receive the gift of ministry.

5

MINISTRY TOGETHER IN DISCIPLESHIP

Sharing of Servanthood in the Church

TWO WORDS sum up the vocation for which God has brought us into being as covenant-sacrament-community. These key words are *ministry* and *discipleship.* In this chapter we shall examine the meaning of our Christian calling in the light of these two cardinal ideas.

Before we begin this exploration, however, we need to think about two fundamental principles which are basic to our understanding of ministry and discipleship: (1) In our thinking about and living out our ministry and discipleship, Jesus Christ stands always at the *center.* (2) The church in its fullness provides the *context* for ministry and discipleship as "we accept our mission of witness and service to all people." We consider briefly these two principles.

Centrality of Jesus Christ

Our affirmation of faith repeatedly points to Christ. But what does it mean to say that he occupies the center of our common life? The figure obviously suggests that the community is formed about him, that it can never lose its contact with its center and still continue to be the church. To put Christ at the center means to make the controlling commitments of his life our controlling commitments. How does the New Testament describe these commitments?

• *Identification with God's will.* From first to last, Jesus brought his purpose for his own life into complete harmony with the will of his Father. At his baptism he insisted, "It is fitting for us to fulfill all righteousness." He began his ministry proclaiming the reign of God. He taught his disciples to pray, "Thy will be done, on earth as it is in heaven" (Matt. 6:10). In Gethsemane he prayed, "Abba, Father, . . . remove this cup from me; yet not what I will, but what thou wilt" (Mark 14:36). From the cross he said, "It is finished" (John 19:30).

To claim Christ as center, we must, like him, identify our purposes completely with the will of God. The church professes to do so as a community of believers. It expects the same commitment from every member who confesses Jesus as Lord.

• *Identification with the whole of humanity.* Jesus of Nazareth entered fully into the risks, the joys, and the agonies of our human lot. In so doing he took upon himself, particularly, the burdens of the poor, the helpless, the oppressed. As one of them he became an outcast, a victim of society's way with the unlucky and the weak.

The early Christians, however, saw something here far more profound than the compassion of a remarkably sensitive human being. They saw a revelation of God, indeed an incarnation of God. (Read 2 Cor. 8:9; Phil. 2:5-11; John 14:8-10.) In Jesus, God entered fully into the needs and sufferings of all humanity. The church, which claims Christ as its Lord, is called to the same kind of identification with all humankind.

A total dedication to these two commitments of the Lord himself could radically alter the life of the church as we know it. However, we need to make one other point about the church's being centered on Christ.

• *Christ as the bond of oneness and peace.* The church is truly formed as we respond to God's call through Jesus Christ and consent to follow him as a community of disciples. But our own experience in partial, and divided churches has distorted our vision. We are blind and do not know it. (See John 9:35-41.)

We assume, for example, that the ideal congregation is a company of persons like ourselves. Since the Christian experience of most of us is limited to congregations like that, we do not realize the extent to which class consciousness determines the limits of our fellowship. For a long time we hid that from ourselves. Then H. Richard Niebuhr wrote a classic study titled *The Social Sources of Denominationalism.* Even so, it is only in situations where ethnic differences determine class distinctions that this aspect of our congregational life has become plain to our sight.

Think about your own congregation. To what extent are its members blue collar workers? Professionals and junior executives? People on welfare? Members of the local establishment? Lower middle class? What range of social and economic differences does it include? What is its ethnic composition? Is its membership open to all persons, or limited to one race?

Why do you suppose Disciples of Christ are predominantly white Anglo-Saxons? Why have we made so little appeal to blacks, both before and after emancipation? Why did we reach so few of the ethnics from southern and eastern Europe who came as immigrants to the United States and Canada in the nineteenth century? Why do we have so few Asians or Hispanics in our membership? To what extent do you think the Disciples have realized the essential oneness given the church in the covenant-sacrament of baptism (Gal. 3:26-28)?

The centrality of Christ also defines the character of the peace which the church rightfully enjoys. In most congregations we prize serenity as the highest good in our common life. But we must ask: What kind of harmony is justified in a church centered on Jesus Christ? The obvious answer would be that harmony which arises from our harmony with his supreme commitments. The church can have no peace by pretending that humanity has no problems, nor by an unspoken consent to remain silent on issues which may be vexing or controversial.

It is no light thing to assert the doctrine of the centrality of Jesus Christ in the life of the church.

The Church as Context

The life of a shared ministry to which God calls every disciple of Jesus occurs within the larger life of the church. Our part in this ministry derives from Jesus Christ through the church. We depend on the church for guidance and support. We do our work of ministry, and live out our discipleship through the church. Of course, only a small portion of our mission is fulfilled "in church," for God calls us to work and serve in the world. But wherever we "do our thing" as Christians, we do so as representatives of the covenant-sacrament-community.

We are united, of necessity, to some local company of Christians. Indeed, in the majority of cases, it is some such group which first draws us into its shared life and brings us to the point of owning Jesus as Christ and Lord. In the worship and work of this community God continues to encounter us and empower us.

The church is the arena for the action of the Holy Spirit. In the New Testament, the Spirit was given to the believers in a body and for the body. The gifts of the Spirit are not given for our private satisfaction, but for the building up of the community in its work of ministry. We have no deeper need as Christians than the need for involvement in the life of a believing community.

Every congregation of Christians is an expression, in a particular place and time, of the universal church. Its life and health derive from the whole body, which is the body of Christ, animated and inspired by him. Thomas Campbell stated: "The church of Christ upon earth is essentially, intentionally, and constitutionally one." The fullness of our ministry and discipleship requires the practical acknowledgment of our oneness with the whole church.

We are one with Israel, the people chosen by Yahweh to witness to the world concerning one God, and to provide in time the family of Jesus. We are one with the whole church of Christ across the centuries, without whose faithfulness in worship and witness the gospel would not have come to us. We are one with the church today, in the extent and diversity of its full ecumenical dimensions. We are one with the church triumphant, the company of the redeemed held together even beyond death in the eternal love of God. Without that Great Church, our congregation would not exist.

In actual practice, the life of the Great Church is mediated to us by the particular church, tradition, or denomination to which we belong. For most readers of this book, that is the Christian Church (Disciples of Christ). In nearly every case, devoted members of this church founded our congregation. Through the regions and the general administrative units of this church, we do much of our work of witness and service. Through these units we share in activities for education and inspiration, produce curriculum resources for our church school, publish the biweekly journal *The Disciple,* which keeps us informed about the Christian world, and provide for the education and care of an ordained ministry.

The common practices of our congregational life—baptism, weekly communion, the shape of our worship, our mood as a people—come to us through this particular church. The way in which we understand the Christian faith, and seek to fulfill our mission, we owe to the common mind of the Disciples of Christ. Our common mind is formed by a shared history, the spirit of great leaders, discussion in conferences, and actions of the church's General Assembly.

Moreover, through the Christian Church (Disciples of Christ) we relate to the Great Church. Because the life of this church, as of any denomination goes on in separation from that of other denominations, it is not only partial, but necessarily incomplete. For this reason we work and pray toward the realization of a more complete form of church. Meanwhile we give thanks to God for the understanding of the faith which comes to us through the Disciples tradition. The meaning of our life as an identifiable company of Christians is expressed in the Preamble of *The Design for the Christian Church (Disciples of Christ)*.

Because we cannot fully realize God's intention for our shared ministry and discipleship together, apart from such a community, in the language of *The Design* "we commit ourselves to one another."

With these two fundamental principles—the centrality of Jesus Christ and the church as context for our Christian vocation—we have established the basis for exploring our "Ministry Together in Discipleship." Consider, first of all, the idea of ministry.

Receiving the Gift of Ministry

Often Christians have tended to regard ministry as a distant reality in the church's life. It is the calling of the clergy. It has to do with priesthood, the control of worship. It involves preaching or teaching with authority. When we have a death in the family, or plan to get married, we send for a minister. Also ministry may involve discipline, or reprimand, or even withdrawal of our privileges as members of the church.

Anyone who knows the Disciples very well certainly would not state their understanding of ministry in this kind of language. Yet such patterns of thought are prevalent, and it is difficult to escape them. Some ministers we see on television tend to confirm these impressions. We watch the Pope receiving homage from vast throngs. We observe the enthronement of an Archbishop of Canterbury. We listen to electronic evangelists laying down the law about the gospel.

Such instances perpetuate the image of ministers as a special class of functionaries who stand apart from the rest of us by virtue of their unusual holiness. Actually, however, such impressions are long outmoded. Current theological understanding of ministry, throughout the church, repudiates them. How, then, shall we think of ministry?

Understanding of Ministry

In the New Testament, ministry means service or helpfulness. Two words in the original Greek designate this kind of working. From *diakonia* (dee-ah-koh-*nee*-ah) we get the English words deacon and diaconate. This word meant service in the broad range of its usage in English—something done for another, a menial chore, public service in a government post, an administrative or leadership role. It is not a word peculiar to Christians, but the church took it over from the workday vocabulary of the world and gave it a churchly meaning.

The other Greek word is *leitourgia* (lay-tour-*ghee*-ah) from which we derive our English word *liturgy*. This term designated a benefaction or service to the public—the gift of a park or municipal building, underwriting the expenses of a celebration, financing a cultural or religious event. From this restricted meaning, it gradually came to designate less dramatic examples of public service and private deeds of servanthood. Eventually it functioned interchangeably with *diakonia*.

English versions of the Bible could be more helpful to us in grasping the meaning of ministry if they translated these two words consistently. Sometimes they are rendered as *ministry* and sometimes as *service* (and rarely, in the case of *leitourgia*, as *worship*). If they were always translated as *service*, we could perceive more clearly the centrality and dignity of that term in the apostolic church. Or if they were always rendered as *ministry*, we could see more vividly the loving helpfulness and unpretentious style which characterized the early Christians.

The Christian community is called by God to serve, and its ministry is service. Within the universal church we receive the gift of servanthood (ministry).

For a better understanding of this gift of ministry, it may be helpful to reflect on how ministry functions in the church.

• *The ministry of Jesus Christ.* Ministry begins with Jesus Christ the Servant (Acts 4:27). Appropriating to his own life the word of the great prophet of the Exile (Isa. 52:13—53:12), Jesus reversed the prevailing understanding of Messiah. The Christ of God would be the Suffering Servant, not the avenging warrior or triumphant king. His life was ministry. His death for and with others was ministry. His resurrection was ministry, opening new possibilities of living for all. His ascension "to the Father" means a continuation of ministry (Heb. 7:25).

Jesus Christ remains the supreme minister and model of servanthood. Within the universal church, which imparts the gospel to us, we receive the gift of ministry—the ministry of the Servant Christ.

• *The corporate ministry shared by all Christians.* The living Lord calls us all into the shared ministry of the servant church. He bids us follow, in the world, his way of loving service to all people. "It is enough for the servant," Jesus said, "to be like his Master" (Matt. 10:25). Our shared ministry reaches out in Christlike helpfulness to those whom life has mishandled and hurt, and in mutual concern for one another. It seeks to make known Jesus Christ and his work to the world.

As Christians together we confess Jesus as the Christ, proclaim him Lord and Savior, accept our mission of witness and service, and celebrate his saving acts and presence in the world.

This is the ministry entrusted to the laity, the entire people of God in Christ. It is what is meant by saying that every Christian has a ministry. A better way of putting it is to say that every Christian shares in the common ministry of the whole church. Protestantism has spoken of this as the "universal priesthood of believers." In *The Design,* it is referred to as the "corporate ministry of God's people" (paragraph 90).

Within the universal church we receive the gift of ministry—the shared ministry which we together offer to God, to the world, and to one another.

• *Order and offices of the ministry.* Within the whole company of believers we also speak of offices of ministry and an order of the ministry. In these offices certain qualified persons are "ordered," or to these positions they are "ordained." In the New Testament, several Greek words are used to designate this action. Basically, all of them mean to appoint a person to a task, as an officer or representative of the church. Some accounts of such appointments mention offering a prayer and a "laying on of hands."

An ordained person is commonly called a "minister," meaning a servant. Sometimes the meaning is enhanced by a phrase, such as "a servant of Christ" (Col. 1:7), "a servant of the gospel" (Col. 1:23), or "a servant of the church" (Col. 1:24-25). This emphasis on the servant image of the minister's role also suggests that the early church ordained these persons for a specific function.

The minister is appointed, not to do the service which the whole church is called to do, but rather to equip (or enable) all the saints (the members) to carry out the "work of ministry" to which all are called (Eph. 4:11-12). There are indications in the New Testament writings that the apostolic church used the term "minister" specifically for persons appointed to such an office in the Christian community. While all believers share a common ministry, some are set apart to perform the tasks of a minister.

Across the centuries, Christ has given such ministers to the church, from the apostles and prophets to today's pastors and teachers. Within the universal church we receive the gift of ministry—the work of those who guide and equip us for the service in which we all share.

Ministry in the Christian Church

Within the order of the ministry, the Christian Church (Disciples of Christ) recognizes the office of ordained minister and the office of licensed minister. Into this order the church inducts both men and women whom it considers qualified. Because these persons serve the entire body, not just the congregation or organization which employs them, they are regarded as office-bearers for the church at large. Accordingly, the General Assembly establishes policies and criteria for the order of the ministry, and the regional church joins with congregations involved to authorize ordinations to this ministry. The chief officer of the church is designated general minister and president; the church in each region has its regional minister.

Congregations order the offices of *eldership* and *diaconate* for service within the congregation (*The Design*, paragraph 97). Christians who bear these offices share responsibility for ministry and service within the local company of believers. They are inducted with appropriate ceremony, which in some congregations is called ordination. These ministries are voluntary, not salaried.

In presiding together, or together with the pastor, at the Lord's Table, elders perform a function which in nearly every other church is the responsibility of an ordained minister. The ministry of elders among the Disciples of Christ is virtually a unique development.

In twentieth-century conversations looking toward church union, questions regarding ministry have presented the most difficult issues. This is a strange situation, for two reasons. First, few members or pastors see any problem here. They recognize as a good minister one who serves faithfully at the tasks ordinarily carried by the ordained, who lives a good life, and who helps the congregation fulfill its corporate ministry. Most Christians experience shock when they learn that the ordination of their minister is not universally acknowledged.

The second reason is that, at the time the churches divided from one another, the ordained ministry was not stated as the key issue. True, the Protestant Reformers rejected medieval concepts of priesthood and papacy, and affirmed the universal priesthood of believers. Most subsequent divisions, however, did not center on ministry.

Yet the issue has loomed large in ecumenical discussion. How does the church assure the faithfulness of its ministers to the apostolic witness? How does the church provide nurture for congregations and exercise oversight in matters which affect the health of the whole body? How does the church express its continuity with the whole company of believers, from the apostles to the present?

In churches of the "catholic" tradition, the proper discharge of these functions is entrusted to bishops. Among Protestants, however, recent decades have seen much painful debate in regard to the ordained ministry. Most recently, Christians everywhere have taken a new approach. Instead of starting with the problem of ordination, discussions are focusing on the ministry of Jesus Christ and, subsequently, on the corporate ministry of the whole people of God.

The ideas about the function of ministry expressed above have gained wide acceptance. The current ecumenical approach to this question begins by looking at the ministry of Christ. That we all gladly confess and proclaim. Next, it emphasizes the shared ministry of the whole people. The question then becomes: Do the churches recognize one another's members as truly belonging to the body of Christ? The General Assembly of the Christian Church in 1975 took affirmative action on this question by an overwhelming majority. The nine other churches in the Consultation on Church Union have also done so.

The "Mutual Recognition of Members" provides a basis for a future uniting of the membership of these churches. Then, it is believed, the uniting or mingling of their ministries can occur. Unity comes from Christ, and from the oneness of the people who make up Christ's body. By unifying their shared ministry, they can order one ordained ministry.

What do you think Disciples have to learn from these discussions of Christian unity and church union? What do we have to contribute in regard to our understanding of ministry?

Discipleship as Ministry

Disciples of Christ affirm that within the universal church we receive the gift of ministry in which every member is called to share. In calling us to be his disciples, the living Christ entrusts to each of us a responsible role within the church's corporate ministry. Discipleship, itself, is a form of ministry.

How does our discipleship express our common ministry? We may explore this idea by reflecting on different dimensions of the name *disciple.*

• *Disciples as followers.* When the first disciples left their fishing nets, their offices, and their homes to follow Jesus, they did not know where he would lead them. They knew only that they must heed his call. In time, they confessed him as Christ and Lord. As they continued to follow him, after the resurrection, they invited others to follow in "the Way" (Acts 9:2). Now we, also, follow that road.

Following Christ means walking with him in the way of servanthood. It means taking the hurts of others upon ourselves and helping them find healing. It means looking with joy on birds and flowers and the goodness of God's earth. It means living simply and gladly, and prizing human possibilities. It means doing each day's work faithfully as service to God. It means communing with God in prayer, and trying to live the "good life" as persons transformed in the likeness of God.

In every congregation we find some disciples like this. Think of those persons you know who can always be counted on, who go the second mile, who reconcile differences, who speak words of encouragement, who carry on the work of church and community— all because their commitment to Jesus Christ orders the pattern of their lives.

• *Disciples as learners.* Jesus came among the people of his day as a wandering teacher, or rabbi, offering the invitation: "Come . . . and learn from me" (Matt. 11:28-29). In our learning, as disciples of Jesus, a study of the Bible holds top priority. Here we learn of Christ and of the God whom he most fully revealed. Serious Bible study requires the use of such aids as commentaries and Bible dictionaries.

Faithful disciples also follow a discipline of study on all matters pertaining to the Christian life and witness. They learn about the church, its work, its teachings, its history. They enlarge their experience by gaining an understanding of other peoples and cultures. They grow in spirit through coming to know literature, the arts, and the sciences.

Good disciples manifest a concern for and a knowledge of current human problems. Residents in a cluster of church-related retirement homes manifest a remarkable demonstration of discipleship which began long ago. They hold study groups in international relations, social problems, literature, and other topics. They go on tours for study of the church's work overseas. They write letters to newspaper editors, give speeches, and write articles and books. In their sixties, seventies, eighties, and even nineties, they are still learners, still disciples.

• *Disciples in community.* We begin our discipleship, and live it out, within that community of disciples called the church. Within this fellowship our lives are mutually enriched and strengthened.

Whether we can trace our faith through the generations, or come to it as the first believer in our family, we are still sustained by the ministry of many other disciples. Through them the gospel has come to us not only in words, but in life. By joining with them we grow in our discipleship.

These followers of Christ form a community of shared commitment in which our loyalties to him are sharpened. They provide a circle of Christian friends. They call on us for help, and they help us in return. They forgive our failures, and receive our forgiveness. They stand with us, and support us, when the crises of life come upon us.

Discipleship Made Visible

The metropolitan culture in which many of us now live calls for a kind of discipleship that perhaps was less needed in the past.

In the nineteenth century, the United States and Canada were still predominately rural. Most people lived on scattered farms, in villages, and in small towns. One's circle of acquaintances was small, but relationships were continuous and often deep. For example, everyone for miles around Bethany knew Alexander Campbell, and he knew them. Issues of right and wrong centered mainly on one's own way of life, and one's dealings day by day with one's family and neighbors. Everyone else knew how one decided. In these relationships, the quality of one's living was a public witness. Often an entire community was profoundly influenced by the goodness or faithfulness of a single disciple.

Today, by contrast, we live in an anonymous urban setting, with hundreds of casual acquaintances, but very few deep and continuing relationships. This is far different from those earlier days as portrayed on television in the 1970s by *The Waltons* or *Little House on the Prairie*. Our lives brush but briefly those of a few persons at work, a totally different set of people in our neighborhoods, still different groups in our political, social, and cultural activities, and a still different company in our church. Often we can go to a concert or a ballgame, where thousands are gathered, and not see a single person we recognize except the players.

Lost in the lonely crowd, we may wonder whether anyone is personally affected by a decision we might make in matters of right and wrong. Most of them will know nothing about it. So many of our relationships are impersonal. In our anonymous society, how does a life-style of personal discipleship make any impression?

Although the individual is often invisible in society, groups of people are readily seen. A congregation, or a task group of Christians, may model the meaning of discipleship in a way that makes the Christian witness visible. Consequently, it is increasingly important for congregations, classes, and families to provide a supporting fellowship for individuals who seek to live out their commitment to Christ. Discipleship is made visible by the life of a community.

The call to follow Jesus holds before us a vision of the possibilities for a meaningful life. It leads us into joys and satisfactions we may not otherwise know. However, our decision to follow him may also expose the depth of our selfishness and cowardice. Like Jesus' first disciples, we may fail at times to measure up to the demands of discipleship.

The call to discipleship is not an invitation to delude ourselves about our likeness to Christ. Rather it is a summons to walk with the best person we can imagine and to recognize at the heart of his goodness a grace which accepts us despite what we are. The forgiving Christ always sees the finer possibilities in us, challenges us to live up to our potential, and gives us the strength to go on. This is his constant ministry to his disciples.

Nowhere do we experience God's grace more intimately than in the fellowship of Jesus' disciples assembled at the Lord's table. Here in receiving bread and cup, and in offering them to one another, we share our ministry together in discipleship.

For Reflection and Discussion

The role of the church as a servant people of God in the world is the focus of this chapter. In the light of this discussion, what would you perceive to be an ideal congregation?

What do you understand to be the "mission of witness and service to all people" entrusted to the church? What is the significance of recognizing the centrality of Christ in the life of church?

In what respects does the church provide a context for fulfilling the mission to which God called us?

How do you respond to the idea that every Christian is called to share in the common ministry of the whole church? What opportunities does your congregation offer its members for participating in this shared ministry?

What is your understanding of the function which the ordained minister is appointed to perform? In what ways may the minister and the laity cooperate in conducting an effective ministry of witness and service through the church?

How would you describe the understanding of ministry as viewed by Disciples of Christ? In what respects does the Disciples practice reflect a concept of a shared ministry?

What suggestions would you offer in regard to ways a Christian, in today's society, might manifest a commitment to Christ as a responsible disciple?

In what ways can a congregation provide a supporting fellowship for its members as they seek to live out their commitment to Christ?

In the bonds of Christian faith
we yield ourselves to God
that we may serve the One
whose kingdom has no end.
Blessing, glory and honor
be to God forever. Amen.

6

KINGDOM WITHOUT END

Freedom in the Will of God

C HRISTIANS pray daily, "Thy kingdom come." Repeatedly, we use for God and for Jesus Christ a language of authority which we would not think of using for any other. We confess Jesus as Christ and Lord. The covenant binds us to God. Our baptism into Christ involves us, through the Holy Spirit, in a life of servanthood (discipleship) and obedience. In the bonds of Christian faith we serve God in the kingdom without end.

Such language bothers many people. It seems to affront our freedom and integrity as persons. We may ask if such expressions are mere vestiges of those authoritarian eras when monarchs were absolute, and God was projected in their image. Would it be better to give up Jesus' image of the reign (kingdom) of God and pray rather for the democracy of God?

What about the church itself? Has it not often used power arbitrarily, even cruelly? Was not the call to freedom a major theme in the origins of the Disciples of Christ, and an important factor in their rapid growth on the American frontier?

Freedom is still a significant issue. It is a central element in our witness as Disciples. Something about the gospel itself awakens in us a commitment to liberty. We roundly affirm with the apostle Paul that "where the Spirit of the Lord is, there is freedom" (2 Cor. 3:17).

How, then, are we to understand and deal with the Christian language of transcendence which attributes sovereignty to God and lordship to Jesus Christ? Obviously, we have to rethink the nature of divine authority. It is not the same thing as the power exercised by earthly rulers (Matt. 20:25-26). Like every other aspect of the divine nature, it is to be understood finally in light of the cross.

Nature of Divine Authority

Primitive religion thought of God as powerful and vengeful. Ancient Greeks pictured Zeus seated among the self-indulgent gods on Mount Olympus. Easily offended, he retorted by hurling thunderbolts at the culprits. Such behavior was standard practice for deity, and parts of our Bible picture Yahweh engaged in this divine exercise.

Christians have often thought along these lines. James and John, for example, wanted to call down fire from heaven on an unfriendly village. The seer of Patmos pictured the triumph of the church in bloody images; at the end all the hosts of evil are to be cast into the lake of fire, and then Christ will begin his reign. Christians sometimes use such scriptures to justify cruel and vindictive conduct. History tells of too many persons made cruel by religious zeal who exercised authority in God's name to torture and kill dissenters.

Such behavior totally misunderstands the divine nature as revealed in Jesus Christ, and our responsibilities under God. It tragically fails to comprehend the movement of biblical thought. Alexander Campbell, in a sermon on "The Progress of Revealed Light," discerned an increasing fullness of divine revelation in the succession of covenants which God made with his people. For Christians, Jesus offers the supreme revelation of God.

Jesus repudiated those primitive notions of God as always achieving the divine will by a show of irresistible force. He could liken God to a king or a judge, but he did not interpret every disaster as a divine retribution for someone's sins. He did not see God as

84

pushing people around. On the contrary, Jesus revealed God as waiting and suffering in patience, like the father of a prodigal son. Supremely, in his own suffering and death, Jesus revealed the awful willingness of God to be hurt by human folly and sin. The only power Jesus had was that of a suffering and ridiculed victim on a cross. God is like that.

If God simply steps back and lets us have our way, does not coerce us or compel us to do right, what then do we mean by divine authority? God's authority operates primarily in two ways: (1) by the law of consequence in a moral universe, and (2) by the attractive power of goodness and truth. Both of these modes of divine action totally respect human freedom.

The law of consequence simply affirms that we are free to choose our actions, but we are not freed from the results of those actions. If we choose to walk off a cliff, we do not keep walking at the same level; we plunge to the bottom. We may choose to build a house on the sand, because it's nice to be near the water; but when the flood comes, the house floats down the channel. Sometimes our choices result in suffering for innocent persons. In such cases, this law may seem heartless. Yet it is an unchanging aspect of this universe.

The law of consequence operates also in the moral realm. Inhumanity arouses inhumanity. Vengeance begets vengeance. Injustice and exploitation breed resentment, until it explodes in revolution and the oppressor becomes the victim. Self-indulgence leads to weakness of character and of body. In our personal lives, our own foibles and sins can strain relationships with those we love, resulting in loneliness, fear, remorse, and misery.

If we do not respond to the danger of suffering the consequences of our actions, and God does not coerce us, what recourse does God have for turning people from folly to truth, from sin to righteousness? The second aspect of divine authority is the attractive power of truth and goodness. This principle was manifest when the followers of Jesus confessed that this powerless, bloodied victim of the world's inhumanity is both Christ and Lord.

All the world's wisdom, and all theologies of divine omnipotence, were turned completely around by the cross and resurrection. God's authority works in our lives not by hurling thunderbolts to make us dance in obedience. Rather, Jesus insists on purity of motive as well as of behavior, a quality of goodness that represents our deepest desire. This kind of goodness arises from our response to the life, teachings, and death of Jesus (John 12:32).

The authority of God is the power of the cross to break the love of

The authority of God is the power of the cross to break the love of sin within us, to melt our hard hearts, and to draw us in love toward a forgiving God.

Religious News Service Photo. The Resurrection, *wood-carving by Elly-Viola Nahmacher.*

sin within us, to melt our hard hearts, and to draw us in love toward a forgiving God. We give our love freely, and seek to do God's will for our lives. The gospel "is the saving power of God . . . because here is revealed God's way of righting wrong, a way that starts from faith and ends in faith" (Rom. 1:16-17 NEB).[1]

The authority of God, as we stated before, totally honors our human freedom. This authority functions in us as we freely respond to God's will according to our best understanding. Indeed, when we honestly confess our highest commitments, we describe our God. By confessing Jesus as Lord we acknowledge that for us the truth and goodness we see in him will have priority in our lives.

This kind of divine authority is what Paul Tillich, a prominent theologian, referred to as *theonomy* (being God-governed). Jesus called it the reign of God, the kingdom which is always ready to break in. Its one necessary condition is our free response to God's initiative. This is what is meant by making covenant.

Authority in the Church

As we think about authority in the church, we need to remind ourselves that the covenant-community is called by God to embody the meaning of the gospel for all to see. Any exercise of authority in the church, therefore, should make clear to all concerned the nature of God's authority. It should demonstrate how completely God relies on the attractive power of truth and goodness, and how highly God values human freedom.

Unfortunately, the church, in the exercise of authority in its institutional life, has tended to fall into one of two false ways. Each of these has emerged, in the church's history, as a reaction against the evident inadequacy of the other. In choosing one or the other of these horns of a false dilemma, good men and women have demonstrated how easily Christians may, for the sake of the highest causes, deny the central revelation of the cross.

God's reign *(theonomy)* depends on freely given human consent to the will of God. But the church has often resorted to either (1) coercion *(heteronomy),* or (2) self-rule *(autonomy).* Even in the service of God's kingdom, these alternatives for the rule of God really deny the gospel.

---

[1]From the *New English Bible,* © 1976. The Delegates of the Oxford University Press, Inc., and The Syndics of the Cambridge University Press, 1961, 1970. Reprinted by permission.

• *Coercion.* In many religions, as well as in secular institutions, leaders tend to exercise authority and power. Although Jesus said, "It shall not be so among you" (Mark 10:43), it did not take the church long to conform to the conventional pattern. Even while it was a persecuted minority, the church excommunicated heretics, cutting off from itself persons whose theology it deemed incorrect. When it became the official religion of the Roman empire, it called upon the police power of the state to banish false teachers.

Even after people stopped persecuting one another over religion, the church hung onto the practice of heteronomy—government by an outside force. Bishops and church courts insisted on ruling the house of God and casting out those who would not conform. Many of the early settlers of North America came to these shores as religious refugees. Barton Stone and Thomas Campbell both defied church courts, insisting on the freedom to preach what they honestly believed.

Coercive authority, or heteronomy, often attracts good people and idealists. The more intense their commitment, the more ready they are to reach for levers of power. Sometimes, we must confess, even the best of us fall into this trap, determined to force on the whole church what we believe is right. We must recognize, however, that whoever wields the power, for whatever good cause, heteronomy is still coercion. It denies God's way of exercising authority in respect for human freedom.

• *Self-rule.* A classic device for escaping the power of hierarchy is to establish a church where "we can govern ourselves." For many early Puritans, congregationalism was the only viable option for setting up a church which was genuinely reformed. Some of them had experienced such bitter encounters with ecclesiastical tyranny that they refused to tolerate any churchly structure beyond the congregation. A large section of Protestantism in England and America came to believe intensely in congregational self-government. Many persuaded themselves that this polity is based on the New Testament.

The growth of congregationalism, however, took an ironic turn. Arising in protest against coercion in the church, it began as a device for ensuring the rule of God within the local company of Christians. Bound by a covenant, these dissenters insisted that a congregation of believers under the lordship of Christ is competent to function as a true church. It could administer the sacraments, provide its own ministry, and interpret the divine will. But gradually this churchly understanding of congregationalism was lost.

Congregational decision-making, designed as an instrument for assuring theonomy and resisting heteronomy, fell into the strange mold of autonomy, as this term was understood in secular circles. Literally, autonomy means self-rule, or calling one's own signals. About the turn of the twentieth century, congregational autonomy emerged as a standard term for describing the polity of Baptists, Congregationalists, Disciples, and several other denominations.

In popular usage, however, autonomy took on such meanings as: "Nobody can tell us what to do." "We make up our own minds about what we want." "We decide all matters that concern us by congregational vote, and abide by the voice of the majority." One would hardly guess that these statements were being applied to a church.

No reference here is made to the sovereignty of God or to the lordship of Christ. No suggestion of praying, "Thy kingdom come." No indication of a sense of covenant relationship with God. Simply, "We decide."

Strangely enough, neither heteronomy or autonomy provides for the freedom of every individual. Only theonomy leads to the total freedom which the covenant-community offers.

A Community Under God's Rule

The church differs from other communities in one key respect. It prays, "Thy kingdom come, thy will be done." It expresses a desire for God's reign to take over, both in its own life and in the life of the world. No one compels Christians to pray thus. But whenever people do pray for the triumph of God's will, there is a true church.

Such a community exists when its members freely choose God's rule (theonomy) over the rule of others (heteronomy) or self-rule (autonomy). This is a body of people who have complete integrity. They have integrity as a Christian church because they acknowledge God's sovereignty and integrity as a human community because they act freely in their commitment to the highest they know. Kept by the covenant, they are yielded to God.

The polity of the Christian Church (Disciples of Christ), as set forth in *The Design,* attempts to exercise authority after the divine pattern. It is the persuasive authority of truth and goodness at work among a people covenanted to do the will of God. The church operates on the principle of mutual consent within a common commitment. No one can make anyone else do anything. There is no way to require a member or a congregation, or a regional or a general administrative unit, to take a particular action.

Some people question whether a body, which lacks such power, can really be called a church. Others believe that such a polity provides the only kind of action proper for a church. This polity seeks to imitate and exemplify God's action in dealing with us.

Nevertheless, authority does operate within this polity. But it is not authority over someone else. The General Assembly of the Christian Church (Disciples of Christ), for example, makes decisions only on matters that affect its own witness as a manifestation of the church. It approves resolutions which express its judgment as to the will of God in particular matters. Yet the power of that judgment is persuasive only, not coercive. Any member, or any unit of the church, may dissent in love.

The General Assembly adopts policies for the general life of the church. Putting these policies into effect requires the assent of the regions, congregations, or boards of the administrative units involved. The only persons who are required to follow the mandates of the General Assembly are the members of its staff and its elected officers.

The principle of authority to act in one's own sphere, without exercising domination over others, operates through the life of the entire church. The General Board and its Administrative Committee act only within clearly defined limits. They have no legal or coercive power to impose their decisions on anyone else. Regions function in a similar way. Congregations exercise the right to make decisions pertaining to their internal life, but they do not order their members what to do.

The Design for the Christian Church (Disciples of Christ) makes no provision for expelling a congregation, and most congregations have no provision in their bylaws for excommunicating a member. The assumption is that the majority of the church will remain faithful to Christ on all essential issues. But that faithfulness will not be enforced by anyone except that individual's own free response to Christ.

A crucial test of this principle of mutual consent arose while the Commission on Restructure was still shaping the original *Provisional Design* for the church. It occurred at the height of the racial crisis when cities were burning and emotions were running high. A demand was made for a clear declaration that no congregation could refuse membership to any person on grounds of race and keep its status as a recognized congregation in the Christian Church.

Here was a clear-cut moral issue which required action. Yet the proposed *Provisional Design* specifically stated that each congregation would have the right "to determine in faithfulness to the gospel [its own] practice with respect to the basis of membership." The only option the Commission had, if this right of congregations was to be respected, was to remind them of the covenantal relationship and their responsibility to manage their affairs "under the Lordship of Jesus Christ." (See *The Design,* paragraph 84.)

After a prolonged struggle, the Commission proposed an additional item in *The Design* to the list of responsibilities of congregations. As amended, paragraph 85 now reads: "Among the responsibilities by which congregations voluntarily demonstrate their concern for the mission and witness of the whole church [is] the responsibility . . . to grow in understanding that the church is a universal fellowship, transcending all barriers within the human family such as race and culture."

That may not sound like much. Nevertheless, it clearly sets forth the principle of mutual consent as it operates in the fellowship of the Christian Church (Disciples of Christ). Congregations may be persuaded to act in a particular manner, which the majority regards as God's will for the church, but they cannot be coerced.

Nowhere in *The Design* do the technical words which we have been using appear. It makes no reference to heteronomy (rule or control by another), yet it rejects all forms of coercion by asserting the principle of mutual consent. It does not speak of autonomy (self-rule, or deciding what we want to do). Rather it affirms our responsibility to make all decisions under the lordship of Christ. Theonomy (God-rule) is not specifically mentioned, but in encouraging reliance on the persuasive power of truth and goodness it exemplifies God's own dealing with humanity.

A Vision of God's Reign

Imagine what it would be like to live in a world totally submissive to the rule of divine love. A vision of such a glorious possibility was the very heart of Jesus' teaching. He called it God's reign, the kingdom of God. He pictured a radical transformation of every person's life, of every human relationship, of the order of society itself. The coming of God's kingdom would bring a reign of righteousness and truth. Love for God and for every human being would transform life on earth into total harmony with the divine will.

The early church, motivated by this vision, continued to shape its life in preparation for the coming of the universal rule of Christ. Across the centuries, this vision has inspired the church with hope for the world. Christians still pray, "Thy kingdom come."

Worship has always been a powerful social force in human history. We hold up before God, through sublime music and transcendent language, the supreme goals of our common aspirations. Believing that these objectives for our life together come from God, we profess them in a vocabulary of ultimate concern.

Strangely enough, a religion that seems other-worldly often exercises remarkable power in changing the present human situation. For example, when black slaves would sing "I Gotta Robe," in anticipation of a heavenly reward, this vision of a final equality among "all God's chillun" inspired them with a personal dignity which transcended the limitations of their earthly lot. Also, the preoccupation of medieval faith with visions of Paradise, where all injustices are corrected by the righteous rule of God, kept motivating Christians to remedy injustices on earth.

In the political realm, a dictatorial regime literally becomes uneasy when poverty-stricken Christians meet in church, even though they are allowed only to sing hymns and read the Bible. The gospel concerns itself with the poor. It celebrates the work of God in casting down the mighty from their thrones. It holds forth the threat and the promise of God's reign, which is always about to break in on a sinful world.

Christians in colonial New England thrilled to the expectation of the coming millennium, a thousand years' reign of Christ. Alexander Campbell looked to the conversion of the world as the preparation for Christ's reign. He named the journal he edited *The Millennial Harbinger,* herald of the kingdom. To get ready for the coming of the kingdom, Campbell labored to evangelize the world and prayed for Christian unity. He believed that oneness among Christians was essential to the conversion of the world.

Campbell's view of the millennium was not other-worldly. Its political and social aspects included democratic government, free universal public schools, personal and social morality, the broadening of higher education, and the Protestant work ethic. It would also bring about the elimination of all superstition, and the end of all oppression—both civil and religious. He saw the increase of justice and equality in the social order as evidence of the gospel's positive influence and promise of Christ's coming reign.

It was these more secular aspects of the millennial hope for the reign of Christ in history which inspired much of the evangelism of the nineteenth century. Revivalists who took the lead in the rapid growth of churches in America included many of the foremost Christian intellectuals and social activists of the time, women as well as men. Proclaiming the gospel of the coming kingdom, they provided motivation for such down-to-earth reforms as abolition, temperance, women's rights, the spread of education, and outlawing of child labor.

By the twentieth century, Christian advocates of social hope were less inclined to use the old millennial language. It had been taken over largely by the "premillennialists," who despair for this world and focus their hope on the end of history, brought on by the Second Coming of Christ.

Disciples of Christ, as well as most Christians in the "mainline churches," continue to share a vision of a social order reformed or transformed according to the biblical witness. Some base their message mainly on the teachings of Jesus and the Hebrew prophets. Others find their inspiration chiefly in the pattern of Jesus' life, and his identification with the poor and oppressed. Others proceed mainly from the doctrines of creation and incarnation, God's intention for and involvement in the world through Jesus Christ.

Some Christians speak of the social demands made on us by the church's sacraments. Still others continue to find the chief impetus toward justice in a vision of the End (eschatology) and God's final judgment on our present evil society.

Which of these several biblical emphases seem to offer the strongest motivation for accepting and pursuing our Christian social responsibility? They are all part of the one gospel. Whichever view seems most convincing, together they project a vision of God's reign which offers hope for the world.

Millions of Christians will long remember the address in 1964 by Martin Luther King, Jr., in which he cried: "I have a dream!" Indeed, that dream will continue to haunt and inspire all of us until the world is set right.

The Church's Task

The mission entrusted to the church includes the call to evangelize, to get out the good news to the world. Obviously, the gospel must convince the minds and change the hearts of individuals as it awakens faith and inspires persons to confess Jesus as Christ and Lord. Those who respond will come not only to receive the Savior's grace for their personal lives, but also to enter into covenant with fellow Christians

93

and with God, to live in obedience to the divine will for the world.

To fulfill its mission of witness and service to all people, the church seeks to hold the good news before the world in various ways. The ministry of the word is a means of witness: preaching, teaching, quiet conversation, and discussion of a Christian approach to specific issues. Service is a means of witness: caring for the lonely and disheartened, feeding the hungry, counseling the confused and distressed. Involvement is a means of witness: taking one's place with the outcast, listening to their hurt and anger, struggling alongside them to right some particular wrong.

Worship, also, is a means of witness: praying "Thy kingdom come" whenever the community is assembled, acting with God to bind new believers, through baptism, in covenant loyalty to God's future, and pausing at the Lord's Table to renew the covenant which unites us with Jesus Christ in his concern for human needs.

Dedication to the church's mission prompts a Christlike devotion. It lifts the vision of congregations from their own immediate concerns to the needs of the whole world. It gives individual members an understanding of church with worldwide dimensions. It motivates denominations to identify more closely with the purposes of God and to explore ways of working together at a common task.

As early as 1849, the Disciples of Christ began organizing agencies to take the gospel to people overseas as well as to minister to the needs of persons in our homeland. Eventually we came to recognize that this ministry of witness and service was an integral part of the church's work, just as truly as were the efforts of local congregations. With the adoption in 1968 of a *Provisional Design* for the church, we began to operate as a total church through three manifestations: congregational, regional, and general. Each manifestation shares in the church's mission, and the efforts of all are essential to its fulfillment.

Much of our witness and service as a church today, both at home and overseas, is carried on ecumenically (in cooperation with other denominations and united churches around the world). Conscious of sharing a common calling, we seek to work with other Christians as partners in mission. In this way we attempt to express God's purpose for the church in the world as we join Christians everywhere in praying, "Thy kingdom come."

Love Beyond Time

Wherever the gospel is preached, and hearts respond in love for

Christ, the reign of God breaks through. Some aspect of Jesus' life and teaching inspires a commitment which motivates an effort in society to correct some ancient evil.

In our society human slavery has been outlawed. Many forms of cruelty, which were once legalized, have been abolished. Minorities have achieved a new measure of dignity and some progress toward equality. A new concern for care of the earth has evolved and many seek more simple and less destructive forms of pleasure. A vocal minority, convinced of the futility of war, struggles to find rational and constructive ways for dealing with disputes among nations.

Meanwhile, however, new evils constantly erupt. Sin and selfishness continue to manifest themselves in the structures of society and in our own lives. It is still difficult to believe in human progress. A readiness for God's reign seems as remote as in Jesus time. Only by faith can we affirm the power of divine love to persuade rebellious human wills and to bring the ultimate triumph of God's reign.

Still, the New Testament bears moving witness to faith in God's final victory. The resurrection of Jesus, our crucified Lord, is our sign that goodness and love will prevail at last.

To the mind of the early Christians, a part of God's victory is the defeat of death itself. In this life, to be sure, the power of the risen Christ brings us new life, the capacity to begin again, a present victory over sin and the "living death" in which evil entraps us. Eternal life begins now. The New Testament faith celebrates this "newness of life," but it also abounds with fleeting pictures of a great host of the redeemed gathered about the throne of God.

The life everlasting is given through the goodness, power, and love of God. It is the manifestation of God's triumph over the last enemy, death. It represents the ultimate harmony of the whole created order in perfect accord with the divine will. It holds before us a vision of hope which motivates us to a complete trust in God, whether in life or in death.

It is this vision of God's ultimate triumph which engages our imagination whenever we assemble about the Lord's Table. Here we look back to the life Jesus lived among us, and we look forward to the great reunion when all those who have loved God are gathered in the eternal presence in perfect harmony with the divine will. It is no wonder that "we celebrate with thanksgiving" this supper which offers a "foretaste of that festal joy."

This victorious faith impels us to "yield ourselves to God that we may serve the One whose kingdom has no end." Because it sustains us in life and in death, it is the faith we affirm.

For Reflection and Discussion

What is your perception of the reign of God as revealed in the teaching of Jesus? What do you envision as the ultimate outcome of God's reign?

In what ways may individuals manifest an acceptance of God's sovereignty over their lives? In what respects does God honor our freedom to choose and act as we please?

What do you understand to be the basis of authority in the church? What suggestions could you offer a congregation which seeks to manage its affairs under the lordship of Christ?

What do you consider to be the primary task of the church as it seeks to fulfill its mission in the world? In what ways may individual Christians help to advance the church's mission of witness and service?

Across the centuries Christians have never ceased to pray, "Thy kingdom come." What image comes to mind when you voice this petition to God? In what ways are you attempting to "serve the One whose kingdom has no end"?